W9-CEC-700

ESCAPE *the* TRAP

Help for Perfectionists and Those Who Live With Them

RICHARD WALTERS

PYRANEE BOOKS

Zondervan Publishing House
Grand Rapids, Michigan

Escape the Trap
Copyright © 1989 by Richard P. Walters

Pyranee Books are published by
Zondervan Publishing House
1415 Lake Drive, S.E.
Grand Rapids, MI 49506

Library of Congress Cataloging-in-Publication Data

Walters, Richard P., 1935–
    Escape the trap : help for perfectionists and those who live with
them / by Richard P. Walters.
        p.   cm.
    "Pyranee books."
    ISBN 0-310-42571-9
    1. Perfectionism (Personality trait) 2. Perfectionism
    (Personality trait)—Religious aspects—Christianity. I. Title.
    BF698.35.P47W35   1989
    284.4—dc20   89-8921
                                                          CIP

Unless otherwise noted, all Scripture references are taken from the
Holy Bible: New International Version (North American Edition),
copyright © 1973, 1978, 1984 by the International Bible Society.
Used by permission of Zondervan Bible Publishers.

All rights reserved. No part of this publication may be reproduced,
stored in a retrieval system, or transmitted in any form or by any
means—electronic, mechanical, photocopy, recording, or any
other—except for brief quotations in printed reviews, without the
prior permission of the publisher.

Edited by Linda Vanderzalm and Nia Jones

Printed in the United States of America

89   90   91   92   93   94   95 / ML / 10   9   8   7   6   5   4   3   2   1

Thank you, Lord,
for your mercy and grace,
which make possible
the healing
of our lives.

Contents

1

Are You a Perfectionist?

Perfectionism is a trap that takes away freedom and strangles enjoyment.

CAUGHT IN THE TRAP

The pain caused by perfectionism could be heard in Ashley's voice as she told me about her husband, Brian. "All he does is work—nothing else. Where are all the good times I used to look forward to? We don't have any good times anymore because all he does at home is read his stupid engineering books!"

Brian defended himself by saying, "You think I work eighty hours a week because I want to? No! But my field is changing so fast that if I don't keep up, I'm history—as valuable to my company as a buggy whip on the space shuttle."

I asked, "How much do you read compared to other engineers at your plant?"

"At least ten times as much, but so what? I only scratch the surface. I could easily miss the very thing I need to learn. I should be studying now instead of talking about it."

"What about the effect on your family?"

"They should be happy—I'm doing it all for them."

Brian and his family were trapped by his perfectionism.

Clarise told her pastor she was unsure of her salvation. When she was a child, she pledged never to drink alcohol, and she had honored that pledge for many years. Then at a wedding reception she drank some punch that contained champagne—a fact Clarise hadn't known when she drank it. For a year Clarise felt guilty about it, confessing it many times in prayer and asking for forgiveness. But she was never sure that she was forgiven. "I enjoyed the punch," she said, "so perhaps I'm not really sorry about drinking it, and I can't guarantee that I won't make the same mistake again. So maybe God can't forgive me. I can't sleep, and I can't think about anything else."

Clarise was trapped by her perfectionism.

Darwin sat in my counseling office complaining about his wife. "You never saw such a neatnik," he growled. He watched me closely, a tense grin on his mouth. "She irons my socks. She keeps a newspaper under the cuckoo clock. I got up in the middle of the night for a glass of water, and when I came back, she had made the bed!"

He laughed and then his tone changed. I heard in his voice a despair that could have come only from an aching heart, "The thing that blows my mind is that she says she takes such good care of the house because she loves me— and I know she does. She wants everything perfect, but there's only one thing perfect in my life now—she has become a perfect nuisance." He put his face in his hands and quietly sobbed.

Darwin and his wife were trapped by perfectionism.

WHAT IS A PERFECTIONIST?

Perfectionists are people who believe they must think and act without flaw, often scolding and punishing themselves when they don't meet this unattainable goal. This approach to life leaves a trail of frustration and breeds only more problems. Perfectionists remember the past with regret, don't enjoy the present as much as they might, and usually dread the future.

If you are trapped by your own perfectionism, this book will help you understand how you got in this trap and offer you the keys to get out. If you are trapped by the perfectionism of someone close to you, this book will describe ways you can help the perfectionist without getting trapped yourself. If you wish to raise children who are free from perfectionistic demands—theirs or yours—this book will help you all out of the trap.

ARE YOU A PERFECTIONIST?

It astonishes me how many people describe themselves as perfectionists. Maybe they describe themselves that way hoping people will think they are more dedicated to achievement and hard work than others are. If they see themselves as perfectionists, they are already at risk; they can easily get caught in the deadly trap.

I hope you try to do and be the very best you can be. Working toward excellence is a good thing. There's not much difference in quality between excellent performance and perfection. But there's a tremendous difference in *what happens to people* when they pursue perfection instead of excellence.

Perfection can't be attained in this lifetime. The person who seeks to be perfect is always doomed to fail. At best, the compulsive pursuit of perfection reduces performance and enjoyment. At worst, it can drive a person bonkers.

INVENTORY FOR RATING PERFECTIONISTIC TRAITS

First, let's find out about your perfectionistic traits. The statements in table 1 describe attitudes and feelings all of us may have at various times. Read each one and decide how much it applies to you. Circle the number that best describes how you usually think. Remember, there are no right or wrong answers.

When you have responded to each statement, transfer the number you circled for each statement to the proper box on table 2. Add up totals for each column.[1]

Table 1
INVENTORY OF PERFECTIONISTIC TRAITS

Circle the number that best describes how you usually think. Don't think too long about each one; circle your first response.

	disagree	agree	strongly agree
1. When I begin to do something, I think about the possibility of failure.	0	1	2
2. As I look back on my life, I remember more failures than successes.	0	1	2
3. My parents gave me rewards (money, treats, privileges) for getting good grades.	0	1	2
4. The results of an activity are more important than the activity itself.	0	1	2
5. People who don't try to achieve their best should be ashamed.	0	1	2
6. I shouldn't let others see me fail.	0	1	2
7. Successful people are more worthwhile.	0	1	2
8. It's normal to get upset over mistakes.	0	1	2
9. I describe my mother as a perfectionist.	0	3	5
10. The best way to achieve well is to set extremely high goals.	0	1	2
11. It's not necessary to make the same mistake twice.	0	1	2
12. People think less of people who fail.	0	1	2
13. People who don't try, don't deserve respect.	0	1	2

14. When I try something new, I expect to fail at it for a few times before I'm successful and that's okay. 0 1 2

15. People who use their abilities deserve more rewards than those who don't. 0 1 2

16. If a thing is worth doing at all, it's worth doing right. 0 1 2

17. Punishment for failure is good because it makes me try harder. 0 1 2

18. I describe my father as a perfectionist. 0 3 5

19. I sometimes think I should work very hard to do my best, whether or not I want to. 0 1 2

20. If I mess up, I should be quite concerned about it. 0 1 2

21. People will like me more if I'm successful. 0 1 2

22. I should do better than average. 0 1 2

23. It's good for me to criticize myself for my mistakes and weaknesses because then I'll try harder. 0 1 2

24. People who make foolish mistakes in public are usually laughed at. 0 1 2

Table 2
SCORES FOR INVENTORY

QPP scores	TSF scores	AOP scores
1. ☐	2. ☐	3. ☐
4. ☐	5. ☐	6. ☐
7. ☐	8. ☐	9. ☐
10. ☐	11. ☐	12. ☐
13. ☐	14. ☐	15. ☐
16. ☐	17. ☐	18. ☐
19. ☐	20. ☐	21. ☐
22. ☐	23. ☐	24. ☐
total	total	total

Using the Results of Your Inventory

The inventory is an index of your ideas about three issues. In general, the lower the score, the more congenial your beliefs; the higher your score, the more likely you are to have problems with perfectionism. The three issues are:

- **QPP (Quality of Personal Performance).** If your score is above 8 on the QPP, you probably expect/demand high-quality performance from yourself. You try very hard because you believe it's important. If your score is quite high, you probably expect/demand perfection from people around you and probably have problems in relationships because of those expectations.

- **TSF (Treatment of Self after Failure).** If your score is above 8 on the TSF, you probably react poorly to failures—remembering them, believing them to be almost inexcusable, and criticizing yourself harshly for them. You probably find that the more you're anxious about your failures, the more your performance will be reduced by interference from that anxiety.

- **AOP (Attitudes of Other People toward performance).** If your score is above 8 on the AOP, you probably are very sensitive to the opinions of others, are strongly motivated to please others (although you may be resentful while doing so), and expect other people to be harsh and critical in judgment. If your score is quite high, you probably have problems managing your anger.

Beneficial Bad News

A problem defined is a problem half solved, some say. If you were honest as you went through the inventory, you have taken a strong step toward defining your problem with perfectionism—if you have a problem.

You may or may not be trapped by perfectionism. But if you are, you're still okay. You just need to put the problem in front of you so you can fix it and put it behind you. If something in your life needs to change, it needs to change, that's all. It's no big deal unless you ignore it and it grows into a major problem.

Finding out that you need to change may seem like bad news, but it's beneficial bad news. The good news is that you *can* change. And this book is designed to help you take steps toward making those changes.

Many chapters in this book will include activities to help you apply the chapter's insights to your own situation. I encourage you to do these activities carefully and with an open mind.

APPLICATION

1. To start, ask God to help you learn from this book. You may want to use this prayer:

> Dear Lord, creator and master of all that is in heaven and earth, I praise you for your sovereign control, and I thank you for your perfect love that generously surrounds me. Because you love me, I dare to ask for your help. Please help me learn what I need to learn about myself so that I can think and act in ways that conform to your ideal. Make me aware of my sinful desires, foolish ideas, and selfish acts. Help me see those as sin, as you do, so I can turn away from them. Thank you for assurance of your pardon as I repent and for the instruction and support of the Holy Spirit as I try to live in the pattern of your perfect Son, my Lord and Savior, Jesus Christ, in whose name I pray. Amen.

Expect God to answer your prayer. The understanding will come—not in the mailbox but in a "still small voice," which often speaks through the impressions that form in your mind under the shaping of the Holy Spirit. Don't be impatient for vivid answers, but move steadily with your study, knowing that God will use many means to teach us.

2. Identify friends who know you well and can express their care for you with sensitivity. Then ask one or two of them to help you answer questions like these:

    a. Am I hurting myself with perfectionistic striving? Am I hurting you? Others?
    b. Do I set realistic goals for myself?
    c. How does my perfectionism interfere with my relationship to you? To others?

Does it take courage to ask these questions? Maybe. But listening to the answers takes even more courage.

2

Perfection and Excellence

Everything was perfect in the Garden of Eden until Adam and Eve sinned. As a result, the relationship between humans and God was broken, and the world was cursed (Gen. 1:1–3:24).

WHAT IS PERFECTION?

We have some understanding of perfection. We find some activities that let us think we have done something perfectly—solving a mathematical equation or crossword puzzle that has one "perfect" solution. But we have merely been correct, not perfect.

A bowler may have a score of 300, a "perfect" game. Or an Olympic judge may give a gymnast the maximum score of ten, a "perfect" performance. But even these situations don't require the highest level of perfection imaginable. For example, a "perfect" baseball game is one in which every batter on one of the teams is retired in order: twenty-seven up, twenty-seven down. At this point in major league history, only fourteen "perfect games" have ever been played. In September, 1988, Tom Browning pitched a "perfect game" for the Cincinnati Reds against the Los Angeles Dodgers. He struck out seven players and didn't go to three balls on any batter. This spectacular display of control was the first "perfect game" in the National League in twenty-three years. But wouldn't that "perfect game" have been more "perfect" if Browning had retired every batter by strikeout and had thrown no balls? Our minds can conceive of ways in which this rare "perfect game," one of the most incredible events in the world of sports, might have been more "perfect."

Now we all know when we say, "Isn't this perfect weather!" or "My, what a perfect baby!" we're describing attainable perfection, not the highest conceivable perfection. We know that absolute perfection is impossible. Well, most people know it.

Perfectionists, however, foolishly believe they can reach the impossible. They believe they can—and must—be perfect. Brian wanted to have a perfect supply of information in his professional field. Clarise wanted her actions and thoughts to be morally perfect. Darwin's wife wanted her house and everything in it to be perfectly neat all the time.

LIVING IN AN IMPERFECT WORLD

However, perfectionists will always be frustrated because we live in an imperfect world. None of us can escape that reality. The Bible warns that "If we claim to be without sin, we deceive ourselves and the truth is not in us" (1 John 1:8).

Even though we can't attain perfection, we seem to have a built-in desire to recreate the flawless harmony of the Garden. We yearn to have harmony in our environment as well as in our relationships—to our self, to others, and to God. We spend our energy trying to attain harmony in these four domains, some investing wisely and others making foolish choices.[1]

But the reality of sin pulls us toward disruption and disharmony. Although we want to live in a harmonious environment, we know that weeds grow in our lawns and our socks get dirty. Although we want harmonious relationships, we are often separated from people by our jealousy, our pride, or our anger. Although we want to have a pure relationship to God, our sin separates us from him.

It's right and healthy to try to restore the conditions God created. God's directive to take dominion of the earth is a mandate to work toward harmony with the environment. God's directives in Scripture point us to a living pattern that allows us to have satisfactory, though not perfect, harmony with people. And God's plan of salvation through the life, death, and resurrection of his Son, Jesus Christ, allows us to be reconciled to him.

This quest—trying to restore the completeness of original creation—can be beneficial to us. We often find exhilaration in pursuing difficult goals. The processes of work, self-discipline, and human relations can be gratifying. We must realize, though, that in this life we can reconstruct only an imperfect approximation of God's perfect order. If we carved a four-foot log into a model of the Statue of Liberty, it might be beautiful, but it wouldn't be the original. We can't recreate the Garden of Eden in this sin-broken world. We may achieve excellence, but not perfection.

However, perfectionists won't settle for excellence. They strive for perfect performance in every area of life and regard the gap between performance and the ideal as a personal failure. They scold themselves harshly and try harder, only to repeat the cycle of impossible demand, discouragement, failure, and self-condemnation once again.

PERFECTIONISTS CHOOSE A PAINFUL WAY TO LIVE

Why do perfectionists do this to themselves? Without realizing it, they are deeply influenced by mistaken beliefs about the world, people, and God. Perfectionists believe that perfect performance, and only perfect performance, will bring them praise and rewards or allow them to avoid criticism and rejection.

There is nothing wrong with wanting to receive praise or avoid rejection; praise is important emotional nourishment, and protecting ourselves from rejection helps preserve our identity and sense of achievement. But perfectionists hold many unhealthy, bogus beliefs, and these bogus beliefs trap them into perfectionism. We'll examine some of those bogus beliefs in chapter 3.

THE SKIMPY BENEFITS OF PERFECTIONISM

Perfectionists think their approach to life will bring them benefits. It does, although the benefits fall far short of the costs. The following statements were made by clients who were in counseling for relief from their perfectionism.

1. Perfectionism emphasizes quality by creating dissatisfaction with mediocrity.
2. Perfectionism is motivating, challenging me to do something better than anyone else does it.
3. In some tasks, like intricate scientific work, there can be no success at all without striving for perfection.
4. A job well done brings a sense of satisfaction.
5. Perfectionism often brings praise from other people.
6. The best worker usually has the most security and best pay.

THE MASSIVE COSTS OF PERFECTIONISM

That's the good news; now for the bad news. After balancing the costs against the benefits, perfectionists invariably say that their perfectionism isn't worth it. The following statements are typical observations perfectionists make.

1. I'm always telling myself I should have done better or I ought to try harder. Perfectionists are never satisfied. They spend great energy wishing they had done differently, regretting they hadn't performed better, and putting themselves down.

2. I often frustrate warmth and friendliness in my relationships. Perfectionists are vulnerable to developing rigid and legalistic attitudes. Because of their internal pressure to succeed, they try to simplify their lives by putting the world into tidy little sets of facts and rules. Most of the world doesn't stand still long enough for that to work. Perfectionists lose flexibility, and that makes human relations difficult. Because they fear people will reject them for their "imperfections," they are reluctant to be known and are defensive to criticism. Perfectionists are often lonely.

3. I have problems dealing with people who don't have the ability to do as well as I can do. Perfectionists want others to be perfect too. Being very critical of their own work, they quickly become annoyed with others' poor performance. As dissatisfaction with their own performance grows, they are likely to start voicing their criticism of others.

4. As a perfectionist I usually don't enjoy doing anything just for the sake of doing it, even something like paddling a canoe. Perfectionists want to measure, rate, evaluate, and compare. They are highly attracted to tasks, but the task must be measurable so they can find out how well they did.

I once took a friend on his first backpacking trip and chose a moderate overnight excursion on the Appalachian Trail near us in northern Georgia. Our plan was to hike about six miles the first afternoon and six more the next morning. My friend checked the map every twenty minutes or so, taking great delight in our steady progress. After a few hours he exclaimed, "Rich, if we keep going at this pace, we can finish up tonight and go back to Athens." Yeah. But that isn't the point of a camping trip, except for a highly task-oriented perfectionist.

5. I have been rejected by friends after I did well on something. Perfectionists' high standards make some people uncomfortable and other people envious. Envy is part of the "cost of competence." It can bring real injustice and problems but is somewhat unavoidable for top performers.

6. Perfectionism is very time consuming. I race the clock constantly, but I never have enough time. Families often grumble about this slavery that erodes relationship. Chapter 13 offers help for people who live with perfectionists.

7. I worry about being able to do what I set out to do. Perfectionists worry about lots of things: their performance, what people will think of their work, even how much they worry! That's a constructive concern. Worry kills. Combine worry with the workaholism that perfectionists frequently develop and you face a complex problem.

8. I put things off. I know I won't be satisfied when I'm finished, so I don't even want to try. Perfectionists are world-class procrastinators. These two problems—perfectionism and procrastination—can nibble production down to nothing. Chapter 11 gives methods for dealing with procrastination.

9. One of my children is just like me—never satisfied with anything she does. If an influential parent is perfectionistic, the child is almost certain to be. Children may develop their own perfectionism through other means, but it's easily passed from parent to child, especially to the first-born child. Chapter 14 offers ways to avoid passing the problem on to one's children.

10. The pressure of being at my best all the time is unbearable. The cost of this kind of internal pressure is remarkably high. Research shows that the pressure of perfection causes performance to go down. Let's examine a task for which a perfect performance would be rated 100. We agree that no one can perform perfectly, so the highest, humanly attainable score is 99. We have two competitors: Eddie, who is capable of a 99, and Frank, who is capable of a 92. Eddie says to himself, *I'm going to get a 99. Nothing less will do.* What Eddie doesn't realize is that his anxiety about doing well will reduce his ability by 12 points. Afraid to achieve anything less than perfection, Eddie gets an 88. Frank, on the other hand, says to himself, *I'm going to do my best and be happy with that. I'm going to enjoy doing the job and be pleased with whatever score I get.* Frank, less capable but also less anxious, is able to do his best and gets a 92. He may even "play above his head" and get a 97. The benefits of perfectionism are more illusion than reality; the costs are real.

11. I feel lousy all the time. Of course! Perfectionists try the impossible, fail, scold and punish themselves for failure, and try again. That's enough to leave anyone depressed, angry, pessimistic, and panicky.

PERFECTIONISM AS A LIFESTYLE PROBLEM

Perfectionism lives in a family with some ugly relatives. The family name is Obsessive Compulsive. Some of the kinfolk are in pretty bad shape—much more distorted than perfectionism.

In the official definitions of mental disorders, much of what this book describes as perfectionism fits within a pattern called the obsessive-compulsive personality disorder.[2] This condition can become quite disruptive—a more serious malady than this book teaches about—and should be given attention by qualified professionals.

A smattering of perfectionism doesn't qualify as an emotional disorder. It is like a common cold: inconvenient, annoying, burdensome—but not a life-or-death issue, not a hospital case, and not a condition that requires a trip to a doctor. But, like a cold, perfectionism lowers resistance to other problems and can turn to something debilitating if it doesn't get better. Perfectionism is worthy of respect and care.

The extreme problem seen in the family is called obsessive-compulsive disorder. The prominent feature of this disorder is recurrent obsessions or compulsions. *Obsessions* are unwanted thoughts that intrude again and again. They often are quite unpleasant and frightening, such as an impulse to kill, a belief that one is contaminated by germs, a fear of failing to turn off a gas stove, or recurrent blasphemous thoughts. *Compulsions* are repetitive behaviors used to neutralize or ward off some dreaded event or situation, but the compulsion either is not connected with that situation or is excessive. An obsessive-compulsive person may wash his or her hands forty times a day or check the stove fifteen times before going to bed as a means of dealing with the persistent thoughts. These obsessions or compulsions cause marked distress and interfere with the person's normal routine. Obsessive-compulsive behavior can often become severe, accompanied by depression and anxiety.

This book will not attempt to address the complexities of obsessive-compulsive disorders. If you suspect you suffer from obsessive-compulsive disorders, you should consult with a qualified specialist in your community.

EXCELLENCE—AN ALTERNATIVE TO PERFECTION

We don't have to be caught in the painful, vise-like trap of perfectionism. There is another way—the way of excellence. And striving for excellence is substantially different from striving for perfection, as is shown in table 3 on page 23.

We often build our lives on *doing,* but God emphasizes *being.* While we spend our energy in trying to measure up, he want us to spend our energy in knowing him—the pathway to being all he wants us to be. This, and only this, permits the perfectionist to drop his or her burden of striving for the impossible.

When our emphasis is *doing,* we often experience frustration, burnout, defeat, and fractured relationships. When our emphasis is *being,* we can experience contentment, freedom from defeat, fulfillment, healthy relationships, and gratification of a job well done—all things God desires for us.

Table 3
STRIVING FOR PERFECTION AND STRIVING FOR EXCELLENCE

	Striving for Perfection	Striving for Excellence
Motivating force	fear	satisfaction and service
Life is built on	doing	being
Results of performance	very good	better
Feeling	sense of failure	contentment
Winning is	required for survival	great but not required
Losing is	devastating	disappointing but manageable
Satisfaction	only at victory	occurs throughout activity
Short-term effect on relationships	pleases others	pleases others
Long-term effect on relationships	alienation, discord	pleases others
Price	hard work, stress, burnout	hard work
Controlled by	other people, past and present	the Christian is self-directed within God's design
Life direction based on	safety	God's purposes
Benefit	short-term success	long-term success

The paradox is that when we pursue *being,* we are liberated from the perfectionism trap, and as a result, we often achieve our best *doing*—personal excellence. Excellence will satisfy us, because we will have accepted the limitations of our created capacities for doing. Isn't that great news?

3

The Source of Perfectionism

"All good things must come to an end," the cliché goes. Unfortunately the mirror image of this saying is also true: "All bad things have a beginning." We look now at how this bad thing, perfectionism, begins.

Our behavior is motivated by our yearning to return to the completeness and harmony that existed before Adam and Eve sinned and were expelled from the Garden of Eden. The yearning for restoration of that ideal condition is the force that motivates human behavior; it's why we act. The particular way in which we act is determined by what we believe; beliefs guide our actions.

Actions, in turn, change emotions and situations for better or worse. Therefore, to improve emotions or situations, we must begin by changing beliefs and the ways we use those beliefs.

HOW BELIEFS, ACTIONS, EMOTIONS, AND SITUATIONS CONNECT

Let's examine a simple case study to illustrate how beliefs, actions, and feelings are connected. Glenn recently graduated from law school and is preparing to take the admittance exam to practice law in his state. He's heard that fewer than half of those who take the exam pass all sections of it the first time they take it. He believes, however, that if he doesn't pass the first time, he doesn't have the ability to be a competent attorney. Let's see how this faulty belief influences him.

1. Belief: "If I don't pass all of the exam the first time, it means I'm not talented enough to be a successful attorney."
2. Emotion: Strong fear.
3. Action: He studies hard.
4. Emotion: He's very anxious when he takes the exam.
5. Situation: Because of his anxiety, Glenn isn't at his best taking the exam, but he passes several sections with strong scores. He looks only at his failure, not at his success.
6. Belief: "I don't have a future as an attorney."
7. Emotion: Painful disappointment, fear of the future.
8. Belief: "I'm no good."
9. Emotion: Shame.
10. Belief: "My friends won't want to have anything to do with me now because I'm a failure."
11. Action: Glenn avoids his friends.
12. Situation: He doesn't receive support at this time, even though he desperately needs it.
13. Emotion: Depression.

Glenn slides into the pit of depression in thirteen quick steps. One belief affects his actions, which in turn affect his emotions and situations. When Glenn started with a bogus belief, trouble was inevitable.

Let's compare Glenn's experiences with those of Hugh, who started with a different belief:

1. Belief: "If I pass *part* of the exam the first time I take it, I'll realize that at this stage in my career

I'm as competent as the attorneys out there now. I'll accept my scores and go on to great success."

2. Emotion: Concern, a manageable level of anxiety about the difficult exam he will take.
3. Action: Hugh studies hard.
4. Emotion: He expects to do well when he takes the exam.
5. Situation: He passes several sections with strong scores and takes great delight in this success.
6. Belief: "I'm on schedule to fulfil my goal of becoming a competent attorney."
7. Emotion: Appropriate pleasure and confidence in the future.
8. Belief: "Hugh, you're okay."
9. Emotion: Contentment.
10. Belief: "I can't wait to tell my friends the good news."
11. Action: Celebrates with his friends.
12. Situation: Receives support and encouragement.
13. Emotion: Confidence and enthusiasm.

There goes Hugh! Some of his friends think he'll be governor some day.

BOGUS BELIEFS

Bogus beliefs are the crumbling foundation stones on which the wobbly tower of perfectionistic striving is built. Glenn built a great deal of his life on a bogus belief. And he paid a big price. That's the way it always goes. It's not possible to build a solid house on a flimsy foundation (see Christ's illustration in Matt. 7:24–27).

Bogus beliefs shape our attitudes toward our self and others. These attitudes spawn emotions, usually unpleasant ones, which influence the development of new beliefs, often other bogus ones, which in turn shape decisions about actions, these likely to be harmful ones.

The bogus beliefs that lead to perfectionism have one thing in common: they are extremes. That doesn't surprise us because in striving for perfection, we are attempting to be the best of the best or to reach the highest of the highest—to attain the extreme. These extreme positions fall in several categories: all-or-nothing thinking, shoulds and oughts, and extreme consequences. Let's consider each category.

ALL-OR-NOTHING THINKING

All-or-nothing thinking requires a person to hold either one extreme position or the opposite extreme position—it ignores the multitude of variations in between. For example, if I were to tell you that when I was in Toledo last Saturday, I met an obnoxious person and therefore have concluded that everyone in Toledo is obnoxious, you would consider my viewpoint quite unfair and mistaken. Rightly so. We know it would be silly to judge all people in any city by the behavior of one person.

The fact is, I was in Toledo last Saturday and talked with about a dozen people. They were all very pleasant to me. But, even with a sample of twelve good experiences, I'm not willing to assume that *everyone* in Toledo is pleasant all the time. There must be grouches somewhere in Toledo; I just didn't meet them.

Our experiences usually fall somewhere between extremes. But it's easy to assume that what is true for the small sample in our experience is true for a whole population that is too large for us to measure.

Another reason we use all-or-nothing thinking is to simplify life. Extremes—like black and white—are easy to tell apart. We aren't likely to have difficulty identifying a white car from a black one but what about shades of gray? We could find thousands of different shades, I suppose. We could have two cans of gray paint so close in shade that it would be impossible for us to say with certainty that one is the lighter and the other the darker. So we may say, "Let's simplify life by forgetting about gray and deal just with black and white."

In reality, however, this doesn't make life simpler because gray does exist. We can't ignore that. In fact, we're involved with gray in life much more than with black and white. Instead of pretending gray doesn't exist, we need to develop our skills for reading tones of gray.

The perfectionist is much too busy to bother with that. The struggle for perfect performance leaves neither time nor energy for the nuances of life.

SHOULDS AND OUGHTS

The second category of bogus beliefs is the shoulds and oughts. In some circles it has been in vogue to judge the words *should* and *ought* harshly and even to recommend that they never be used. Aha! Isn't that a fine example of all-or-nothing thinking? Such a view is an overreaction that would shift the error from one polarity to another.

Wisely balanced shoulds and oughts are necessary for individuals and society. We *should* honor God. We *ought* to set aside money for a rainy day. We *should not* drive through red lights. We *ought not* to throw bottles out the car window. The Bible presents quite a few matters in absolute terms, so orthodox Christians have traditionally believed in shoulds and oughts.

However, perfectionists are unable to keep the shoulds and oughts in balance. They feel bombarded with shoulds and oughts, if not from the people around them then from their own inner demands. Dozens of times a day they hear, "You should do this" or "You ought to have done better than that." They need and deserve release from the tyranny of these commands. Release is available, but it's not found by moving from one extreme to another.

EXTREME CONSEQUENCES

The third category of bogus beliefs common among perfectionists relates to how they perceive the consequences of their actions. They often believe, for example, that if only they could accomplish that perfect goal, then they would be respected, remembered, rewarded, and live happily ever after. That's a nice thought, but it doesn't happen that way. Perfectionists are affected powerfully by fears of negative consequences from their failures: "If I mess up, *everyone will laugh at me forever*" or "If I'm late for work this morning, *I'll lose my job and never work again.*"

Many perfectionists have unhealthy beliefs about the penalties of violating their shoulds and oughts. This was the case with Irv. Irv knew he shouldn't watch pornographic movies. He believed doing so was such an offense to God that he should take literally Mark 9:47, "And if your eye causes you to sin, pluck it out." After he rented and watched a pornographic video, Irv felt consumed by guilt and thought that God would never forgive him. A few days later he poked his eye with a screwdriver, fortunately failing to blind himself. In addition to some psychiatric treatment, counseling by a pastor led him to accurate understanding and joyous experience of God's forgiveness and supportive love.

Many of us base our actions on bogus beliefs, creating a chain reaction of behavior that often leads to trouble. Examine the list of bogus beliefs in table 4 and identify bogus beliefs you perhaps hold.

Table 4
COMMON BOGUS BELIEFS

Each statement reflects one of the bogus beliefs we have explored (A–N refers to all-or-nothing thinking; S/O refers to shoulds and oughts; EC refers to extreme consequences).

Bogus Beliefs About the Environment

The way to get security is to do everything perfectly (A–N).

A miss is as good as a mile (A–N).

Whenever it rains, I know everything will go badly that day (A–N).

Life should be fair (S/O).

This road ought not to be so bumpy (S/O).

If we get caught in the rain, we'll all catch pneumonia (EC).

You'll die within a year breathing the air in that city (EC).

Bogus Beliefs About Self and One's Performance

If I'm criticized, I'm no good (A–N).

My work is my worth (A–N).

If I make a mistake now, I'll do it again and again (A–N).

I ought to be able to do whatever I put my mind to (S/O).

I should never feel bad when I can't do something perfectly (S/O).

If I don't do well, I'll hate myself forever (EC).

It will ruin me for life if I don't get the part in the play (EC).

Bogus Beliefs About People

If I do enough, people will like me or respect me (A–N).

If I don't do enough, people will reject or hurt me (A–N).

If I mess up, no one will like me (A–N).

People ought never to be disrespectful to me (S/O).

People should like me (S/O).

If I goof up in front of them, I'll just die (EC).

Once people know my weaknesses, they'll exploit me without mercy, and I'll suffer forever (EC).

Bogus Beliefs About God

If others don't like me, God won't like me either (A–N).

If I don't perform perfectly, God won't like me (A–N).

If I am less than Billy Graham and Mother Teresa combined into one, I'm not an effective spiritual person (A–N).

God ought to tell me everything to do (S/O).

God should not allow people to hurt me (S/O).

God will send me straight to hell for this (EC).

As soon as he went to that church once, I knew he would never be a healthy Christian again (EC).

Bogus beliefs are the prime movers in perfectionism. Whether these beliefs originated because someone influential said them to us or because people repeated them during our development or because they were said at a time when we were emotionally pliable, they have great power over us. We give these messages great validity and importance. They shout to us in our minds.

I call this the mega-voice because it drowns out the other voices from within and without. The mega-voice drowns out praise by shouting, "You don't deserve it." The mega-voice drowns out laughter by shouting, "Trouble is just around the corner." The mega-voice drowns out silence by shouting, "Get busy; keep working or someone will do better than you."

The mega-voice demands: "Work harder, do more; work harder, do more," drowning out the songs of birds and the whispers of the breeze. It shouts, "Do more, do more," stifling the sounds of love. With relentless repetitions the mega-voice snarls, "Not good enough, not good enough" until even the comforting voice of God is unnoticed, trampled beneath self-condemnation. The tongue of the mega-voice is a whip, prodding and cutting its victims.

But that can change. Instead of trembling at the sound of the mega-voice, you can be soothed by the comforting voice of the Lord. First, you need to hear what is really being said in the conversations of your mind. Use these exercises to apply the lessons of this chapter to your life.

APPLICATION

1. You can't refute your bogus beliefs until you know what they are. Study the examples in this chapter well so you can recognize a bogus belief, then listen for the bogus beliefs that circulate in your mind. Your bogus beliefs will be a little different from any of the examples, but you will recognize them if you listen.

2. Carry a 3″ x 5″ card or a tiny note pad with you to write down examples of bogus beliefs you discover. Add a mark for each time you hear one repeated. Although this will interrupt your routine a little, it won't be as big a nuisance as the bogus beliefs are causing already.

3. As soon as you have time, write a statement to replace each bogus belief with truth—a true view. Example of bogus belief: "Nobody will enjoy what I cooked for supper." A true view to replace it: "This is a delicious meal, and those who like good food will enjoy it. If they don't, it's okay."

4. Learn your true views well enough so that you can remember them the next time you find a bogus belief in your mind. Your goal is not to memorize a list of statements, but to shift to a new way of thinking. At first it will seem a little artificial, but with time, you'll find your thoughts changing for the better.

4

Distorted Understandings or Balanced Beliefs?

Christianity asserts that we may have life and have it to the full. It is so. When Christianity is rightly understood and practiced, people are enabled to break the bonds of sinful nature and move beyond bogus beliefs and confusions that lead to perfectionism and similar problems. God's design for living shows us how to live effectively.

But we all have a tendency to want to tinker with God's design. "The time will come when men will not put up with sound doctrine," Paul wrote. "Instead, to suit their own desires, they will gather around them a great number of teachers to say what their itching ears want to hear. They will turn their ears away from the truth and turn aside to myths" (2 Tim. 4:3–4). Nothing is more dangerous.

In describing distortions that can foster perfectionism, I don't wish to disparage any individuals or church traditions. Rather, I wish to call attention to the importance of knowing the Christian faith and coming to a balance of belief, relationships, and practices so that we can enjoy and celebrate God's intentions for us.

With the goal of clearer biblical understanding, let's examine six distortions that can foster problems related to perfectionism.

SMUGNESS: THE MIRAGE OF MORALITY

Imagine a man standing in front of what he pretends is a full-length mirror, inspecting himself to see if there is any sin in his life. What he looks into is not a mirror but a carefully painted image of himself as he would like to be— perfect. The man postures and preens. He pats himself on the back. He squeals "What a pretty boy am I" and chuckles with self-satisfaction. From heaven God looks at the man, knowing that the gratification he gets from his self-delusion is minuscule compared to what he could have by living humbly and honestly. And God aches for the man to change.

That's imaginary. What about real life? What do you hear in comments like these: "There are only two other churches in this town [of 100,000] that are doing anything spiritually." "There are a lot of good people in that church and they take God seriously and everything, but they won't be in heaven [because they don't believe the same as we do on this issue—about which the Bible is silent]." "It's a shame. They used to preach the Gospel there, but now. . . ." "Since you didn't go to the seminar, you couldn't understand." "I had that problem when I was a baby Christian, but I'm above that now." "The preacher over there quoted from the Bible and two elders fainted."

Isn't it easy to be smug? Perfectionists are prone to engage in "smug talk"—sort of a *smugscreen*—to camouflage their inadequacies. They use smug talk to bolster their self-deception of perfect performance.

Hearing "smug talk" at church, especially from the pulpit, reinforces the illusion that perfection in human performance is attainable. Smugness is the opposite of humility and charity. It may lead to a church-centered subculture in which communication has no more substance than trading pretense for pretense.

LEGALISM: PICKY PIETY

A young receptionist in a medical office arrives five minutes early every morning. Exactly five minutes early. Although time cards are not required, she keeps her own record of when she arrives at work and when she leaves and returns from every coffee break and lunch hour. Without fail she takes one minute less than the allotted time. She keeps the records on her own time, of course!

Her boss assured her that such extreme attention to time was not necessary, but she smiled and said, "I just want to make sure I do my part."

One evening she stayed late to finish some insurance reports, explaining that an unusually large number of questions from patients had interfered with her efficiency. Staying late became more frequent, and within three months she was staying late half an hour or more three times a week. The explanations she offered to her boss always made sense.

But what the young woman was thinking inside doesn't make sense. In the privacy of her mind she believed that she hadn't worked as hard as she could have and she was therefore guilty of cheating her employers. She compensated for her perceived inefficiency by working extra hours. She put this in spiritual terms—if I do less than my maximum, I'm stealing from my employers, and God will punish me for that sin.

In reality she was working very effectively until she began worrying about it. Finally she was able to describe her fears to one of her employers, who gave her this explanation: "Imagine that you are carrying a bucket of water from a faucet to a flower garden. It's a good bucket, and you walk carefully and get to the flowers with all the water. Then you go back, refill the bucket, and make another trip. You make trip after trip this way. Fine. Now, if the bucket gets a hole in it, what do you do?"

36

"Walk faster," she replied.

"Sure. But suppose that worrying about the water that was leaking out could make another hole in the bucket."

"Then I wouldn't want to worry, but I probably would, and I would walk faster just in case."

"Yeah, I think you would. But what might happen if you did?"

"I'd get tired. Also, I might spill some water by walking too fast or maybe even fall down and spill the whole bucket." She smiled as she began to see herself in the parable. "But I want to do well."

"We all know that, and we appreciate that about you. You do some of your best work when you work at a reasonable pace."

"I'm always afraid you won't be satisfied."

"We have been and we are. We want you to be satisfied, too. I think you were happier, weren't you, when you were working at a more relaxed pace and not demanding so much from yourself?"

"Yes, but . . ."

"Enough said."

"But . . ."

"Enough said."

"But . . ."

"I repeat—we have been satisfied and we are satisfied. But we want you to enjoy yourself as much as we enjoy you."

The woman had imposed strict rules on herself because she was apprehensive of authority figures, so she assumed she would receive criticism if her time logs weren't meticulously accurate. The woman transferred these attitudes, the result of early life experiences, to her understanding of God, whom she perceived as a stern police officer. As she accepted greater liberty at work and sought to know God more personally, she gradually found relief from her self-imposed laws. As God wants and asks for our full devotion, he frees us from the legality of the Law.

WORTH BY WORKS: REJECTING THE GIFT OF GRACE

A middle-aged woman says sadly, "I can't understand why the Lord would love me. I was such an awful thing when I was a kid. I'd sass my mom. I was always in trouble. In ninth grade I skipped school and ran off with a boy for a week. But we came back before the money ran out, thank goodness, and I got back in school. It bothers me no end that I still think of those things. I make up for it by reading the Bible a lot and by doing all the volunteer work I can."

When quizzed further about her lifestyle, she makes these comments: "I wonder if I should sell my car and get a cheaper one?" "Next summer I should put in a vegetable garden and put up canned goods to send to the food bank." "I wish I could be in an attitude of prayer all the time, but my mind wanders off, and I think of things of this world too much." "Other people seem to be able to do much more for the Lord than I do. And what I do is so shabby."

The woman expects nothing from God; everything is up to her. She lives not under grace but under laws of her own devising as she attempts through both quantity and quality of service and piety to earn her relationship with God. Because she is her own legislator, sheriff, posse, judge, and executioner, she is under constant duress. When God extends his grace to us, it is as if he says, "The universe, which is mine, is yours now, too. Enjoy. You can work to enjoy it, but you can't work your way into my favor because you're already there."

UNREALISTIC EXPECTATIONS: CRAVING INSTANT PIETY

In contrast to the woman who believes it's all up to her, a pastor exhorts, "Jesus will deliver you from every evil thought, from every craving for sin. You need no longer be lured by the lusts of your flesh. You will have a wall of protection between you and the sinful pleasures of this earth. You will no longer desire the things of this world, and the evil of this world can't harm you."

Sounds great, doesn't it? But it suggests a quick and complete change, which is not a scriptural teaching. This pastor's advice is quite different from the frustration Paul described when he wrote, "The evil I do not want to do— this I keep on doing" (Rom. 7:19). Paul's continuing struggle with inner impulses to do wrong is seen in the lives of other great characters of the Bible. Consider the ups and downs in the lives of Moses, David, Peter, or Timothy.

Several religious traditions have struggled with this issue. The Wesleyan understanding of perfectionism has sometimes led people to expect impossible performance in personal morality or service. Unfortunately, some of Wesley's followers to this day have tried to attain a level of perfection that Wesley himself found tyrannical—a level he denied that he himself had attained.[1] Teaching the unattainable does an injustice to the God-blessed and history-changing tradition of the Wesleyan movement and brings frustration to people who try to follow human expectations that are higher than God's.[2] (For a fuller discussion of the Wesleyan view of Christian perfection, I encourage you to read the article in the appendix.) Similarly, Roman Catholics friends have told me that their tradition, influenced by the ascetics and the abuses of penance, also can lead people to excessive self-denial and focus on works.

Whatever the particular religious tradition may be, misunderstandings can abound. But once people find a balance between faith and discipline, they are freed to live and work righteously rather than resentfully. In our life on earth we gradually achieve moral perfection step-by-step, if we choose; in heaven, we will experience complete moral perfection. Until then, we are diligent strivers who should try to be as charitable toward ourselves as God is toward us.

CRITICAL SPIRIT: THE HOLY HARPOON

In talking about one of his teachers, a high-school boy says, "Yeah, he's a great teacher, like a legless man teaching running. Swift, real swift."

Ten years later he says to his wife, "I know you're only pushing 110 pounds, but how many are you pulling? It's the way you cook. Don't you know anything about nutrition?"

By middle age he can't talk without sarcasm and condemnation. He says of his neighbor: "He'd steal a dead fly from a blind spider. His reputation is so bad his shadow won't walk down the same side of the street with him."

He says to his son: "You blew it again. When will you ever learn to do things right—the way I showed you?"

He says of a co-worker: "I asked that new secretary to take a letter, and she said, 'Where to?' I think her wisdom tooth is retarded." Nobody laughed, and at last he began to wonder why he didn't have any friends, especially within his family.

This man was reaping the consequences of his critical spirit. If you confronted him about his critical approach, he would say, "But nutrition is important." So it is. "And dishonesty is wrong." We can agree. "And a father needs to show his son how to do things." He's right again, but he excessively reacts to failure, over-zealously corrects, and clumsily offers opinions—even if the opinions themselves are accurate.

People with a critical spirit are like the Pharisees: they can strain out a gnat but swallow a camel. Jesus said to them, "Woe to you, teachers of the law and Pharisees, you hypocrites! You give a tenth of your spices—mint, dill and cummin. But you have neglected the more important matters of the law—justice, mercy and faithfulness. You should have practiced the latter, without neglecting the former" (Matt. 23:23).

Jesus conceded that the Pharisees were correct in some of what they were doing, but he took issue with their neglect of the major issues. This is the tragedy of the critical spirit—losing the essentials.

LICENSE: FROLICKING IN DEPRAVITY

A young pastor jokingly says that his greatest public service is snatching fundamentalist ministers from the jaws of self-discipline. Today he is lunching with two pastors from evangelical churches located in his neighborhood. He rests his forearms along the restaurant table, leans toward the two pastors, and quotes Jules Feiffer, "Christ died for our sins. Dare we make his martyrdom meaningless by not committing them?" He watches the other pastors very carefully.

"That might be a bit much," he continues, "but the statement has a point, doesn't it? Our sins are covered, so why worry? Your don't–don't–don't preaching makes people think Christians can't have fun. You put people on a treadmill of piety," he exclaims. "You make *treadmules* out of them. Thank goodness for your feet-of-clay media stars who showed the world how much fun a Christian can have."

Suddenly the pastor sits back, shocked at the bitterness he hears in his own voice. He stammers an apology. The other two pastors shift uneasily, then one of them says, "That's okay. If we're going to know one another, we need to say what we think. You have, and we'll take it in the right spirit. Look, you don't need a license from us to say what you want to say."

License. The word jolts the young pastor with one of its other meanings: excessive or undue freedom or liberty. *Bang!* he thinks, *I just shot myself in the foot.*

That afternoon as he sits in his study, he sees the pile of reference books he had been consulting for a sermon. Yes, antinomianism was the fancy word for the fallacy he had fallen into: that justification by faith and faith alone exempts Christians from keeping the Ten Commandments. Slowly and painfully he began to realize that in reacting to the stifling confines of legalism, he had gone to the other extreme and rejected obedience, the cornerstone of Christian living. He had shackled himself with freedom.

God has given us disciplines for living. Some of them are "don'ts" and some of them are "do's." Each is an expression of his love. License would turn off the traffic lights and tear down the stop signs, and with that greater freedom we would be so much more likely to die between here and the grocery store.

REGAINING BALANCED BELIEFS

Correcting distorted beliefs can begin only after we are willing to admit our misunderstandings and surrender our need to be self-sufficient. We need to remember that it doesn't matter to God that we find it impossible to live sinlessly. He wants us to trust him and enjoy our relationship with him. But we can't enjoy this relationship if we are hung up on rule-keeping legalism, the dishonesty of smugness, or the pride of a critical spirit. Our relationship to him requires candid confession and humility.

We can ask the Holy Spirit to make us aware of attitudes and behaviors that need changing, and we can ask the Spirit to help us make those changes. Quiet times of Bible study and prayer will help us focus on the Lord's will and working in our lives. The legalist will benefit by structure without rigidity: for example, have Bible study daily but not at the same time each day or with the same people. Study alone some days, with a roommate or family member on others, with a small group once a week. A person prone to arrogance will benefit from a support group marked by open confessions and accountability to one another. (Chapters 9 and 10 will describe additional helpful strategies for change.)

Some people attempt to hide from God because they still feel shame (a result of their guilt), although their guilt has been absolved. The way to combat shame is to accept God's grace. People who have problems with guilt and shame usually *understand* grace well enough in their heads; they *know* about justification by faith and the futility of works righteousness. But they haven't incorporated what they know into their lifestyle. They have been pardoned from the prison of sin, free to leave, but they remain in their cells. They choose to remain because they are trying to earn their salvation instead of accepting grace.

I have seen this condition change—radically and dramatically—on several occasions through people praying in thanksgiving for the accomplished fact of God's forgiveness of sins and for his eternal, unconditional love.

The following prayer is a composite of two prayers by women who were liberated from years of shame, self-condemnation, and perfectionistic striving when they *accepted* God's forgiveness, which they had *received* years earlier:

> Dear Father, Almighty God, thank you! You have forgiven my sins! For nearly a year my life has been chaos and confusion. You hadn't forsaken me, but I had separated myself from you. In your Word you say that if we confess our sins, you are faithful and just to cleanse us. I claim this verse and ask your forgiveness in Jesus' name, and seek to receive what you have promised—your forgiveness.
>
> Thank you for this forgiveness, so free for all of us. Thank you for the assurance that you have forgiven my sins and removed them from me as far as the East is from the West.
>
> You give me joy overflowing and a heart filled with gratitude. Help me to grow, to mature in my devotion to you, to serve others. In Christ's name I rejoice in new life and pray this with assurance of your love. Amen.

5

Sorting Out the Problem

The last two chapters have described the source of perfectionism. We have explored the bogus beliefs that influence emotions, actions, and situations, and we have seen how distorted understandings and warped attitudes lead us away from the Christian ideal. Now let's examine a method of dealing with perfectionism in our own lives.

Real life is like a jigsaw puzzle with many pieces; it's complex and can become scrambled. This chapter introduces the diagnostic diamond, a system to help sort out the pieces, learn where the problems come from, and understand how to resolve them.

PERFECTIONISM AND THE DIAGNOSTIC DIAMOND

We have already discussed the interrelationship of beliefs, emotions, actions, and situations. Let's expand the element of belief to include all our cognitive (mental) processes and mechanisms—beliefs, memories, reflection, understanding, creativity, reasoning—and rename the element *intellection,* which will include decision—the moment we quit debating about the options and choose one.

We may not take action at the point of decision, but we have willfully selected an action and made a commitment—both mental and emotional—to take that action. Decision is the end point of the intellection process, the final mental process before action.

Finally, we'll add one other element, this one the most important of all: truth. There is only one kind of truth—God's truth. All that God is, is truth; all that is not of God, is not truth. So it doesn't matter if you describe this as truth, God's truth, God's law, or God's design for living. I like the word *design* because it freshens my awareness that if we will only live as we were created to live—by God's design—things will go the best they can in spite of sin in the world. So let's add *design* to our list.

Now we have *intellection, design, emotion, action, and situation.* The first letters of those words are I–D–E–A–S, a reminder that changing our emotions or situations begins with healthy ideas.

The five elements—intellection, design, emotion, action, and situation—are shown as a five-sided pattern on figure 1. Each element can affect the other. Because of the shape of the pattern, we will call it the diagnostic diamond. It reminds us that life, like a diamond, has many facets; it looks different from different perspectives.

The word *diagnostic* means that the diamond can help us diagnose or find the causes of the problem. The diagnostic diamond can help us find not only bogus beliefs but also conflicts (discrepancies) between one element and another element.

In figure 1, the diagnostic diamond is superimposed on a heart. Why the heart? Because the Bible frequently uses the heart as a metaphor to describe inner processes. For example, the Bible uses the word *heart* 399 times to describe intellection and decision, 166 times to describe emotion, and 257 times to describe the personality in general. Personality simply means the pattern of thinking and acting that is usual for a particular person. The biblical use of the word *heart* links action to our other elements,

Figure 1
THE DIAGNOSTIC DIAMOND

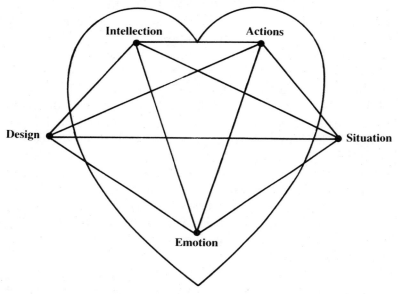

for example, "Out of the overflow of the heart the mouth speaks" (Matt. 12:34).

Notice that *design* and *situation* are outside the heart shape. That position reminds us that design and situation are external to us, although they can affect us quickly and powerfully. (The extent of influence is determined more by what we *think* than by any other factor.)

We can have almost total, direct control over intellection (including decision). It is influenced strongly, of course, by what has been learned and experienced early in life, by genetics, and by those influences subsumed under the "Law of Generations."[2]

We usually have less control over our actions. This may be because we don't have the competence or opportunity to act in a certain way. More often our actions are limited voluntarily. For example, when we take a job to earn money to buy groceries, we exchange some of our freedom for certain obligations. If we make good exchanges, our total amount of freedom increases.

We need to keep in mind that we don't have to *commit* an act to be affected by it. Jesus taught emphatically about this in Matthew 5:21–30 when he described the complications of anger toward another person and when he equated lust with adultery. Strong desires toward sinful action impact our emotions, shape our decisions, and affect the quality of our relationships—whether or not we allow the desire to become an action.

The diagnostic diamond can help us to sort out the many influences that create and encourage perfectionism, and it can guide us toward resolution. Let's look at Jolene's life and see how the diagnostic diamond helps her understand and resolve her struggle with perfectionism.

JOLENE AND THE PERFECTIONISM TRAP

Jolene, a young single woman, teaches fifth grade in a public school. She has a great reputation with her students' parents, but she's not getting along with her principal. Jolene complains, "My life will be worse than horrible until I get away from Mrs. Krane, that monster of a principal I work for. She doesn't like me because I work harder than she does, so she's trying to destroy me by giving me the worst kids in the school. Now I can't sleep or eat, and I'm uptight all the time. No matter how hard I work, I know this job will be the end of me."

Let's sort out Jolene's situation with the diagnostic diamond. Find figure 2 and read statements 1–12 in numerical sequence. Now look at Jolene's beliefs, items 1, 3, 6, 8, and 12. Are any of these bogus? We don't know. Mrs. Krane is probably not a monster, but she may be difficult; we don't know. Does Mrs. Krane want to destroy Jolene? Probably not, but the fact that Jolene thinks so is

Figure 2

JOLENE: PART ONE

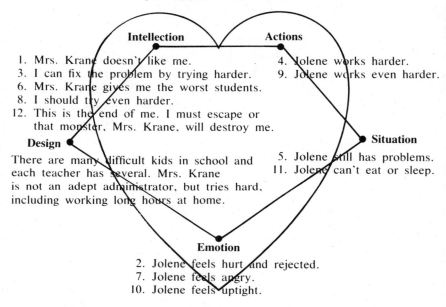

Intellection

1. Mrs. Krane doesn't like me.
3. I can fix the problem by trying harder.
6. Mrs. Krane gives me the worst students.
8. I should try even harder.
12. This is the end of me. I must escape or that monster, Mrs. Krane, will destroy me.

Design

There are many difficult kids in school and each teacher has several. Mrs. Krane is not an adept administrator, but tries hard, including working long hours at home.

Actions

4. Jolene works harder.
9. Jolene works even harder.

Situation

5. Jolene still has problems.
11. Jolene can't eat or sleep.

Emotion

2. Jolene feels hurt and rejected.
7. Jolene feels angry.
10. Jolene feels uptight.

certainly significant. I'm not willing to believe that this must be the end of Jolene, but it must be extremely painful for her to think so.

With encouragement to say more, Jolene admits, "Yesterday I screamed at the kids during class. If Krane finds out, I'm doomed. I hate that woman, and I'm going to bring her to her knees. I only pretend to cooperate with her now. This morning she gave me an announcement to read to the class. I didn't read it, but I told her I had."

This doesn't sound like the Jolene we thought we knew, and we gulp in disbelief. Knowing that she has been active in a church, we inquire about that. "No, I just haven't felt like going any more. I think God doesn't care about me or he wouldn't let all this happen." We hear bitterness in her voice and notice that she clenches her fist as she continues, "Besides, that ugly Krane claims to be a Christian, but I have yet to see anything about her that reminds me of Christ. So why go to church if it doesn't make a difference in the way we live?"

This additional information about Jolene's situation is illustrated in figure 3. As you read this second set of statements in numerical sequence, look for bogus beliefs, conflicts with God's design, and conflicts between beliefs and actions.

Figure 3

JOLENE: PART TWO

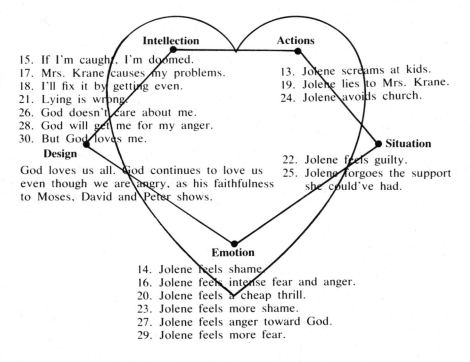

Intellection

15. If I'm caught, I'm doomed.
17. Mrs. Krane causes my problems.
18. I'll fix it by getting even.
21. Lying is wrong.
26. God doesn't care about me.
28. God will get me for my anger.
30. But God loves me.

Design

God loves us all. God continues to love us even though we are angry, as his faithfulness to Moses, David and Peter shows.

Actions

13. Jolene screams at kids.
19. Jolene lies to Mrs. Krane.
24. Jolene avoids church.

Situation

22. Jolene feels guilty.
25. Jolene forgoes the support she could've had.

Emotion

14. Jolene feels shame.
16. Jolene feels intense fear and anger.
20. Jolene feels a cheap thrill.
23. Jolene feels more shame.
27. Jolene feels anger toward God.
29. Jolene feels more fear.

With this additional information, perhaps we can see more clearly whether or not the beliefs are bogus. Is she doomed? Certainly not. She has a big problem, but she's not doomed. And what about statement 17? Mrs. Krane is part of the problem and may be causing Jolene some discomfort, but Mrs. Krane is not the root cause of Jolene's problems. Numbers 18, 26, and 28 are definitely bogus; numbers 21 and 30 are valid.

Are there some conflicts with God's design? Yes. Some bogus beliefs are merely incorrect (15, 17), some touch on moral issues (18), and some contradict truth about God (26, 28).

Jolene has a mixture of bogus and valid beliefs that conflict with each other; for example, she believes that God doesn't care but that he loves her. A contradiction anywhere in the system will generate confusion and discomfort.

We find conflict between her belief that lying is wrong (21) and her action of lying to Mrs. Krane (19). The lie creates guilt. Note in the diagram that the word "guilt" is listed under *situation* rather than *emotion*. Guilt is more than an unpleasant feeling; it is a condition of disharmony in relationship with God. The feelings associated with this guilt—this disharmony with God—are described by the word "shame."

Now if you had been able to talk with Jolene about her situation and use the diagnostic diamond to help her organize her statements, you would have been a counselor to her. A counselor is a special kind of teacher/friend who helps another person resolve emotional, spiritual, or relational problems and learn to live more effectively. When Christians live by God's design, they are often able to be counselors—teacher/friends—to help others.

Now, let's think about how we can help Jolene take care of some of these problems. First, Jolene needs to sort out what she believes about the nature of God and the nature of his relationship to us. In the heat and confusion of emotional turmoil, a lot of ideas bounce around, often conflicting with each other. That's why she needs to sort things out and put them down in black and white. If Jolene were to see figure 3, she would probably want to reaffirm her belief that God loves her and modify statement 26 to say, perhaps, "Right now it feels that God doesn't care, but I *believe* he does. I'll continue to live on the basis of that belief."

Having sorted out beliefs about the nature of God, her anger would probably diminish. She then would find it easier to confess and repent to God about lying, which is the only way to take care of that guilt. Then, when she experienced God's forgiveness, her feelings of shame would disappear. I call this second aspect of the process *accepting* the forgiveness that has been *received* from God; some people refer to it as "forgiving yourself."

Now, suppose later on Jolene offered more about her early life. Find figure 4 and read the statements in numerical sequence.

As you can see from reading figure 4, Jolene's confusion began a long time ago. Although she had learned some true things about God, those beliefs were not balanced by other facts about God's nature. This resulted in her distorted theology: work hard for God or he'll punish you. Jolene's beliefs generated some fear, but she thought that working hard brought enough rewards to neutralize the fear. She thought her system worked.

But it didn't work well enough or completely enough to serve her in the more complex circumstances of adult life. Her fear of God kept her from developing the quality of relationship that would comfort her and bring her moral strength during stressful times.

Confronted with this new understanding, Jolene needs to resolve the underlying issues. First, she needs to confess and repent of her bitter hatred toward Mrs. Krane (she doesn't need to talk with Mrs. Krane about the hatred, but she needs to report the incident of lying and apologize for it). Second, she needs to forgive her parents and other spiritual teachers for the errors they instilled within her (again, she doesn't need to talk with them about it). Third, after realizing that she's been basing her actions on some distorted beliefs, she needs to find the truth—about God and about herself—and act on it. Fourth, she needs to pursue a more personal relationship to God.

Figure 4

JOLENE: PART THREE

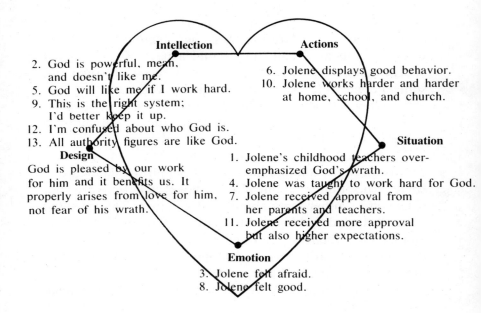

Intellection
2. God is powerful, mean, and doesn't like me.
5. God will like me if I work hard.
9. This is the right system; I'd better keep it up.
12. I'm confused about who God is.
13. All authority figures are like God.

Design
God is pleased by our work for him and it benefits us. It properly arises from love for him, not fear of his wrath.

Actions
6. Jolene displays good behavior.
10. Jolene works harder and harder at home, school, and church.

Situation
1. Jolene's childhood teachers over-emphasized God's wrath.
4. Jolene was taught to work hard for God.
7. Jolene received approval from her parents and teachers.
11. Jolene received more approval but also higher expectations.

Emotion
3. Jolene felt afraid.
8. Jolene felt good.

USING THE DIAGNOSTIC DIAMOND IN YOUR LIFE

You too can use the diagnostic diamond to organize the puzzle pieces of your life. Your purpose is to see the chain of events and discover where your unpleasant emotions or difficult situations are coming from.

First, write the five I–D–E–A–S elements on a sheet of paper, with room for lists under each element. When you begin, put down the first thing that comes to mind. It doesn't matter where you start. Let's say it is fear, so you write that under *emotion* and think about what you thought or did after the fear. If you remember it, write it down; if you can't, no matter. Try to remember what you did just before you were afraid and write that down.

You see that you can move either forward or backward in time. To keep track of the sequence, number each item, beginning with 20 so you can move in either direction.

With the understanding you gain from this discipline, you can take the same four steps Jolene needed to take: first, confess and repent to God and others, as appropriate; second, seek divine healing of trauma or omissions of nurture that have been part of your life; third, replace bogus beliefs with truth; and fourth, pursue growth in Christian knowledge and experience in personal relationship to God through Christ.

LORNE AND THE DIRTY SOCKS

Figure 5 shows how a man named Lorne used the diagnostic diamond to learn how his bogus beliefs led to a tantrum at the dinner table. Lorne began his list with the statement indicated by the bold-faced 20; from there he listed his other insights, indicated by the other bold-faced numbers. (Read the sequence of the bold-faced numbers 20–26.) Lorne first recalled his frustration and irritation in finding dirty athletic socks in the bathroom sink when he got home from work. He remembered grumbling to his wife about it. She had explained that their son, Mort, had been washing the socks himself and that she thought that they should be pleased at his initiative. Lorne thought he had felt better after that, but then he recalled being tyrannical and highly critical at the dinner table and later being ashamed about it.

Lorne decided to begin the diagnostic diamond again to see if he could add details. Read through figure 5 again, starting at item 20 and following the lighter-faced numerals. Lorne realized that in his frustration and irritation, he thought that the family didn't respect him, and he felt angry about it (22, 23). He had the conversation with his wife (24), felt better (25, 26), but now realizes that he had thought, "Everything should go right for me" (27). Finally he reacted with the tirade at his family and subsequent shame (28, 29).

Figure 5

LORNE AND THE DIRTY SOCKS

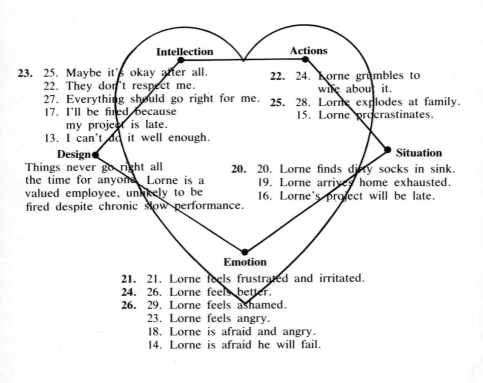

Intellection

23. 25. Maybe it's okay after all.
22. They don't respect me.
27. Everything should go right for me.
17. I'll be fired because my project is late.
13. I can't do it well enough.

Design
Things never go right all the time for anyone. Lorne is a valued employee, unlikely to be fired despite chronic slow performance.

Actions

22. 24. Lorne grumbles to wife about it.
25. 28. Lorne explodes at family.
15. Lorne procrastinates.

Situation

20. 20. Lorne finds dirty socks in sink.
19. Lorne arrives home exhausted.
16. Lorne's project will be late.

Emotion

21. 21. Lorne feels frustrated and irritated.
24. 26. Lorne feels better.
26. 29. Lorne feels ashamed.
23. Lorne feels angry.
18. Lorne is afraid and angry.
14. Lorne is afraid he will fail.

Then Lorne decided to think backward in time. Read those statements in the same reverse sequence that Lorne discovered them. He arrived home exhausted (19). He knew that he had been quite fearful and angry all day (18) because in the back of his mind he had thought, "I'll be fired because my project is late" (17). It was true that his project was late (16), but it was the bogus belief (17) with its extreme consequences that generated his strong emotions.

Why was Lorne late? It was his own fault; he'd been procrastinating. As he thought about this, he recognized considerable fear within himself (14). Prayer and thoughtfulness about that over a period of several days brought him to the very important discovery of his underlying thought, "I can't do it well enough" (13). That's a bogus belief.

Lorne recognizes it as a bogus belief. He has an exceptional track record on the job; he has fulfilled every project—with excellence, but never on time. His procrastination has been as predictable as the fine quality of his work. That belief is definitely bogus.

What other bogus beliefs do you identify in Lorne's intellection? What conflicts do you find between God's design for living and Lorne's actions? What truths need to become part of Lorne's intellection?

Each of us has some bogus beliefs that need to be identified and replaced with truth. We don't need to allow our bogus belief to cause us and others to suffer. Since we can't change bogus beliefs until we find them, it's beneficial bad news when we find one.

I urge you to get out your own pen and paper and begin sorting some of your own puzzle pieces with the diagnostic diamond. I have observed in counseling that every person who has done this with a willingness to learn about himself or herself has learned valuable lessons. You will too.

A Challenge

Jolene had asked, "Why go to church if it doesn't make a difference in the way we live?" It's a good question, one we need to ask too. Cynics have a field day when they look at the performance of Christians. "The last

Christian died on the cross," Nietzsche said. The behavior of Christians is enough to drive Santa Claus to pessimism. Even C. S. Lewis, a man of great love for God and his people, admitted that one of the difficulties he had with Christianity was Christians.

G. K. Chesterton identified the cause when he said, "The Christian ideal has not been tried and found wanting; it has been found difficult and left untried." Jolene made that mistake when she withdrew from worship and fellowship.

Sarcastically, George Bernard Shaw said, "Christianity might be a good thing if anyone ever tried it." Let's try it. Not just dabble, let's really do it. The diagnostic diamond can help you.

6

What Will You Do with Perfectionism?

If you are a perfectionist who wishes to change, you *can* change if you want to. This chapter explores processes that will help you make some of those necessary changes.

BREAKING FREE OF PERFECTIONISM

Even though you will get out of your perfectionism trap in ways different from others, you probably will use some of the same escape routes. I have seen these principles and methods for healing work dramatically for many people. I know they can be useful to you—if you want them to be.

Give careful attention to each part of the process and follow the suggestions in step-by-step sequence unless you have a clear confidence that you should do otherwise. As you seek God's direction, he may orchestrate the change process into a pattern none of us has seen but a pattern that will be exactly right for you. Just be sure it's God who is directing you.

Chapters 6 through 10 offer a systematic process for

breaking free of perfectionistic striving. Here is a summary of the steps:

1. Bring God's resources into the process. The most important part of the process is to seek and accept God's involvement in the reconstruction and healing. God's power is essential because the forces that motivate and energize perfectionistic striving begin so early in a person's life and get so tightly intertwined with everything else.

2. Do you want to be a perfectionist? You can change a major pattern like perfectionism, but you must make an intentional decision to change. Without that decision of your will, you will remain in the perfectionism trap. This chapter will help you face your decision.

3. Discover where your perfectionism began. Where did you develop your perfectionism? You probably have some difficult feelings, attitudes, or behavior associated with the person who led you into the perfectionism trap. Perfectionists often discover anger, rejection, and alienation in their relationship to their perfectionism mentor. Chapter 7 will help you focus on the origin of your perfectionism.

4. Change who you are. This process begins by understanding what is and isn't important to God in his relationship to us. Chapter 8 describes biblical foundation stones on which to build a pursuit of excellence instead of a striving for perfection.

5. Change what you think. You are already on your way to understanding the bogus beliefs that justify and perpetuate your perfectionism. Chapter 9 gives you more help in this and shows you how to improve the quality of your thinking.

6. Change what you do. Healthy thinking often leads to healthy actions, but sometimes old habits pop up again, trying to regain control. Chapter 10 shows you how to stay on track.

Now you have seen the game plan. If you are ready to play to win, I'll stay with you as combination coach and cheerleader.

BRING GOD'S RESOURCES INTO THE PROCESS

It's never easy to change a habit. If it were easy to change, it wouldn't be called a habit. Expect to be frustrated at the unevenness of your progress in breaking the perfectionism habit. Remember that even though three steps forward and two steps back is frustrating, it *is* progress. And at times, you'll even take two steps forward and three back. But be patient with yourself and look to God for help.

If you know that God will supply the help you need, you can be more confident as you face your Goliaths. If you know God as a close personal friend, you have companionship through difficulty. You get this confidence and companionship by talking with God—praying. During your process of change, pray regularly. If you have a hard time formulating prayers, use these for starters:

Pray in praise of God's perfection:

> Great God, creator of all, only you are perfect. I can't even imagine your perfection. But in my limited way, I acknowledge it and praise you. Amen.

Pray in thanksgiving for God's love:

> Thank you, dear Lord, for understanding and accepting me in perfect and total love in spite of my imperfection and wishy-washy love. I know that you hug me to yourself tenderly, wrapping me in your love as a parent does with a child. Thank you for loving me. Amen.

Pray in thanksgiving for God's healing power:

> Thank you, gracious God, for your healing power that helps me move, albeit slowly and incompletely, toward the perfection we see in the life of your son, Jesus Christ. Without your help I lie wounded on the roadside of life; with your healing power, we

walk together. Thank you for your mercy, which brings healing to my wounds. Amen.

Pray for courage and wisdom:

Mighty God, I have been so blind to my needs, so ignorant of my possibilities, and so fearful of change that I have often sat in the corner with my self-pity and confusion instead of coming to you for help. But I come to you now, asking for your help: to discern my condition and its roots, to see truth about myself as you reveal it to me, to be bold enough to try new patterns of living, and to persevere during the time of change. Amen.

Pray in confidence of the answers that will come:

Faithful God, you invite my prayers and I have prayed. I wait, reassured and nurtured by our conversation, confident that your response to my petitions will be in a form that will be good for me. You may surprise me, but I know you won't disappoint me. Amen.

Pray in candor:

Here I am, gracious God, impatient and petulant, grumbling again because things haven't gone the way I wanted them to. I have been angry toward you because like Adam and Eve I have wanted to give orders, not to obey. Forgive me again. Amen.

DO YOU WANT TO BE A PERFECTIONIST?

People become perfectionists by playing follow-the-leader, trailing behind a perfectionist and imitating that person because it makes sense at the time. Perfectionism is a decision, but in the beginning the decision is an unintentional one because it's made without understanding either the implications of the decision or the other choices.

Although you got caught in the perfectionism trap unintentionally, you can get out of the trap only through an intentional decision. I want you to begin to think about that decision now.

Trying to be perfect in what you do, think, or feel has advantages and disadvantages. Is perfectionism worth it to you at this time? Use the chart in table 5 to analyze your answer to that question. As you fill in the chart, consider how striving for perfection affects your *relationships* (with parents, spouse, children, friends), *satisfactions* (quality of life, freedom, enjoyment), *activities* (vocation, school, hobbies, recreation), and *attitudes* (about your self and about the past, present, or future).

List both the rewards and the cost of striving for perfection. The quality and completeness of your thinking are important now. The best way to work on this is to think about it for ten or fifteen minutes at a time on three or four occasions. And don't try to make a perfect list!

Once you have completed your lists, size up the two sides. Where is the stronger sentiment? Are the rewards of striving for perfection worth the costs? Do you want to keep your present patterns or change them? It's your life, so it's your choice.

I won't tell you what to do, but I need to tell you what one woman said after she filled out her chart: "When I suddenly realized that all my hard work wasn't worth it, I felt myself blush. I was embarrassed that I had lived so long with wrong attitudes about work and life. I knew at the time I felt silly, but I was also overjoyed because I had this great sense of permission to quit being a perfectionist. Here was the evidence—in black and white—showing me there was a better way to live. I said to myself, 'Okay Marlys, you can get off your case and begin to live better.' I made the decision to change and what a wonderful difference it made in my life!''

Think about it for yourself. Are you ready for a wonderful change? Or are you comfortable in the perfectionism trap?

Table 5
SHOULD I ATTEMPT TO BE PERFECT?

Yes, because it has these advantages/rewards	No, because it has these disadvantages/costs

7

Discover Where Your
Perfectionism Began

Perfectionism is based on the bogus belief that perfect performance, and only perfect performance, will bring praise and rewards or a shield against rejection and punishments. People who have adopted this bogus belief usually have gotten it from their parents—loving parents as well as indifferent ones. Let's see a couple of examples.

NELS AND HIS SILENT FATHER

Nels, a successful dairy farmer, was severely depressed. "I work hard about 350 days a year," he told me. "I have done this all my life, and I love it. It might seem crazy to you that I could go out to a barn every morning in the dark and work hard until it's dark again and love it, but I do.

"I could quit dairying and do something easier, or not work at all for that matter, but I like what I do. And I would miss it if I wasn't doing it." He rubbed the back of his neck slowly and looked at the ceiling, his brow as creased as a muddy feedlot. "If I could change one thing,

I'd want my dad—just once—to tell me I was doing okay.''

Nels was forty at this time, his father sixty-five. They had worked together since Nels was knee high to a heifer. Nels now owns the farm, and he and his dad work together every day, just as they had for many years. Nels said, ''Not one time has my dad ever told me that he liked anything I did. He's a good man, my dad is, and a man of few words. When I was a kid and would mess up, he wouldn't yell at me or cuss. He would just teach me how to do it better. He was gentle in correcting me, but he never gave me a compliment—not one in all these years.''

''How do you feel about that, Nels?''

''That's just his way. He's a man of few words.''

''So it doesn't bother you that he has never complimented you?''

''No, it's not something I think about.''

''It doesn't bother you.''

''No.''

I think I disagreed with him. What do you think? After all, Nels brought the topic into the conversation, and he had said he would change that if he could. Of course it was important to him.

I said in a matter-of-fact style, ''Perhaps you never did anything to merit a compliment.''

He looked at me, fire strong in his eyes. If he had been a Jersey bull, he would have been pawing the ground with his front hooves, getting ready to make an angry charge. He shouted, ''Of course I have deserved a compliment! Hundreds of them. I have been state Dairyman of the Year, haven't I? Yeah, I deserve a compliment, but what does it take to get his attention?'' With that he began sobbing from the depths of his heart—pain that had been buried beneath twenty, twenty-five, thirty layers of hurt, each layer a year of effort, a year of hoping that his dad would say, ''I'm proud of you, Son.''

Nels cried hard for five minutes or more before he could speak. Then he said, ''I'm so ashamed to be ungrateful about him. He's a good man; he did the best he knew how. I shouldn't be angry at him. I should be glad that he's such a good man."

Nels told a couple of anecdotes about his father, and then I asked, "Where did your dad learn how a father gets along with a son?"

"Just watching his father."

I asked Nels what he knew about his dad's father.

"Grandpa was another hardworking, silent type. I was real young when he died, but I know that's the way he was. Dad is probably a clone. Back in those days, they worked a lot harder and suffered a lot more than now. They didn't have time for small talk. Oh, shoot, I don't know if it's right to talk about this stuff," he said. "I won't push the blame for my troubles onto him."

"Of course you won't, Nels," I said. "And that's not what this discussion is about. Right now you're learning more about your dad's point of view and how it influenced you. It's right and proper, not disloyal or disrespectful. Understanding your dad better will help you enjoy him more, which will benefit you both. It'll help you become more effective in living, which I imagine was one of his goals for you, wasn't it?"

Nels agreed. His strong, meaty hands rested uneasily in his lap. He was not used to sitting for a long time, and he shifted restlessly. His keen mind skillfully sifted through his family history and the many intertwined emotions.

"I think I get it," he said. "I wanted his praise, so I worked hard and I worked smart, expecting him to praise me for it. He couldn't give me the praise because he didn't know how; he'd never had a chance to learn. I felt rejected, and I've been mad at him for it. I didn't admit it because admitting it would make me feel guilty. But it ate at me anyway."

I grinned, delighted at his understanding, and he grinned back at me. "Okay Doc, it's your turn now," he challenged. "What do I do about it?"

Nels' father had done the best he knew to do in

rearing his son. He had not praised Nels because he didn't know how to do that. Nels worked hard to earn praise, but it never came. It was a pleasure to teach Nels about the relief that could come by forgiving his father for those omissions. During the succeeding months as Nels forgave his father, the depression began to lift.[1]

Nels needed to use additional strategies to break free from the bogus beliefs and habits of his perfectionism. It was a long struggle that could be successful only because the underlying problem with his father had been resolved. But he was at last relieved of his depression.

ODELIA AND HER TALKATIVE MOTHER

Odelia was another perfectionist at the end of her wits. She described a mother who was quite different from Nels' silent-type father. "My mom," she said, "talks all the time, and most of what she says is pointing out what isn't perfect about something. She can see fingerprints on the windows of airplanes flying overhead. She's trying to get our parakeet to chirp in the key of G. We went to Mount Rushmore, and she thought Lincoln needed to comb his hair. She just thrives on picky-picky rules. If she'd lived in Jesus' time, she would have been bucking to be the first female Pharisee.

"Not that I don't love her," she added hastily, "which I do, especially after my 'trip to hell and back.' But it's just so hard to get past all her criticism. She has made a career of criticizing. About all I got to say while I was growing up was 'I'm sorry' and 'I'll try harder next time.' I would have liked to say, 'It was pretty hard to do as well as I did, and I'm proud of what I accomplished' or 'I don't think I can do any better,' but . . . well, there just wasn't a place for anything but perfection in her house—"

I interrupted. "I notice you said *her* house."

"Yeah. It was hers—not mine, not ours—hers. Maybe she didn't want it that way, but it was. So I got out of it as soon as I could. Sixteen years old and I hit the streets. A teenage bag lady. Which is when I found out, blast, I'm just like she is. I could have puked when I found that out. I couldn't stand the dirt, I couldn't stand the noise, I couldn't stand the confusion, and most of all I couldn't stand the thought that I couldn't make it on my own and that I'd have to go back to *her* house. So I looked around to figure out what to do.''

Odelia sat tense, hunched over, pressing her knees together with her hands, staring at them. ''Everything I saw was aimless,'' she began slowly, ''and I couldn't stand that either. I decided I needed a purpose. What did I know about purpose? Nothing. My mother's purpose was finding fault. I wasn't going that way, for sure. Money became my purpose. For the next nine years my whole life revolved around making a dollar any way I could, mostly on the wild side. I'm lucky to be alive. I got shot at, beat up more than a few times, but that's the chance you take if you live in the fast lane of the gutter.

''That takes my story to when I was twenty-five years old, with a bunch of dollars stashed away. I was utterly burned out and miserable. I called my mother about going over to see her, which would have been the first time in two years, and she was very excited. I fixed myself up quite dressy and conservative and went to her house. She greeted me and said, 'You're fifteen minutes late.' I started to back off and leave. But I thought, *That's what I would say to her if it was the other way around.* So I stayed.

''We sat and talked, and whenever she bad-mouthed something, I acted like I took it seriously. When I said something more atrocious about it, she would top my remark. She finally caught on that I was mimicking her. I thought she'd blow up, but it struck her funny, and we made a game out of it.

''That's when I decided to turn my life around. I got my G.E.D., went to college, and got an accounting job. I started dating decent guys, and I got married. And what do you know! I was as meticulous around the house as I was as an accountant. I folded my husband's shirts as if I were an origami master, and I put them in the chest of drawers,

67

dress shirts on the debit side, sport shirts on the credit side. Guess what? It turned out he liked his shirts on hangers. So, can you believe this, we decided there was nothing to do but divorce.

"Now I have my shiny, tidy little place. The goldfish swims clockwise on odd-numbered days and counter-clockwise on even days. I level the pictures daily and tune the piano every week. I put one of those paper strips that says 'sanitized for your protection' on the toilet seat after every use. It's a perfect little kingdom, 'where seldom is heard a discouraging word, and the skies are not cloudy all day.' I hate it.

"I'm so picky, people can't stand me any more. Especially me. I can't stand me at all. I wish I'd go away and take my fussy habits with me, but I never do."

THE ROLE OF FORGIVING

It was important for Nels and Odelia to learn where their problem began for two reasons: First, it brought more vivid understanding of their pattern, helping them know what to change; second, they needed to identify the person who influenced their perfectionism so that they could work through their resentment toward the person. As it happened, the influential person in these two cases was a parent, but that isn't always the case.

Nels was trying to be perfect in the hope that his father would open up and compliment him; Odelia tried to be perfect so that her mother would shut up. As they learned where their painful perfectionism had begun, they felt uncomfortable toward the influential parent. The cluster of emotions included disappointment, anger, and shame and fear about feeling angry toward the parent. These feelings and attitudes were not new; they were just coming out of hiding. The discomfort toward the parents would be very damaging if the feelings were allowed to fester and grow. However, when Nels and Odelia were able to forgive their parents for their *imperfection* as parents, the resentment subsided.

As you think about your own perfectionism, you may discover that someone other than your parents influenced your perfectionism. Maybe it was a teacher or sibling or boss. Whether your perfectionism began in or outside your home, you need to face the fact that you can't go back and reshape the past. What has happened has happened. You need to accept the realities of your past and begin to forgive your parents and others for their imperfection.

Forgiving is the only way to relieve the pain caused by wounds received from others, whether the wounds were inflicted deliberately or were the mistakes of ignorance or personality style, as in the cases of Nels and Odelia. If you wish to read more about the healing power of forgiveness, I suggest you read one of my earlier books, *Forgive and Be Free: Healing the Wounds of the Past and Present* (Zondervan, 1983).

APPLICATION

1. Using a sheet of graph paper, draw a history of your perfectionism. Horizontally, at the bottom of the graph, chart your age in five-year intervals, from birth at the left to your present age at the right. Vertically, at the left side of the graph, list several levels of perfectionism, from a low level at the bottom to a high level at the top. Mark the level of your perfectionism at as many different ages as seems important to you; then connect the points with a line. After you have completed your graph, think about the influences that raised or lowered your level of perfectionism.

2. Identify the people who influenced your perfectionism. Did someone teach you to be perfectionistic? Who? Who were your heroes during your formative years? Who were the perfectionists you copied—teachers, parents, pastors, siblings, peers? Why?

3. Pray and ask God not only to make you aware of memories that may be important to your healing but also to help you ignore unhealthy memories. Then ask him to give you the wisdom you lack. He will.

8

Change Who You Are

Perfectionists find their satisfaction in doing things that bring about good situations and pleasant emotions. Now there's nothing wrong with wanting good things. God wants us to find harmony with the environment, with other people, with our self, and with him.

The problem comes from the inept and misguided means we use in trying to find that harmony. We seek the world's goals and use the world's methods. But a world system can never bring *enough* satisfaction.

Charlie Chaplin is still lauded as the funniest movie comedian ever, but as one of his four wives recalled about him, "He had no sense of humor at all; he never found it easy to laugh." Milton Berle, after a sixty-year career making people laugh, admitted he had everything a man could want except happiness. "I am content with my family and my wife and I live very comfortably," he said. "Monetarily, I'm fine. But it's that extra something that I'm looking for . . . that I haven't found yet." Nor did getting laughs bring contentment to some superstar comedians. John Belushi died at thirty-three from drug abuse, and Freddie Prinze took his own life. The world's rewards, without relationship with God, can never bring happiness.

I once saw a list of thirty-six rock musicians who have died from substance abuse or suicide. Were any of them more content than Elvis Presley when he died, apparently from a variety of physical overindulgences? Elvis had assets of $15 million at death. Before he died, John Lennon, one of the Beatles, said, "The Beatles are more famous than Jesus Christ." Maybe they were. (See where fame ranked in Jesus' priorities, Phil. 2:5–13.) Lennon, though murdered, reportedly was anorexic and addicted to heroin at the time of his death. How content was he? Rewards, without relationship with God, can never bring contentment.

A Japanese businessman, Yoshiaki Tsutsumi, is said to have a personal fortune of at least $21 *billion* dollars, yet he has been described as a penny-pinching Scrooge. In talking about his hobby of photography, Tsutsumi has said, "My problem is the film. If I have three or four shots left, I agonize over whether to get a roll developed or to use it up. In the end, I usually get it developed, but only after a huge struggle." Does it seem to you that his immense wealth has brought him freedom? Without a relationship to God, no amount of the world's goods can bring freedom.

The world's way can't satisfy. To be content, we need to be reasonably fulfilled in each of the four areas (environment, others, self, God), but if personal relationship with God is missing, no amount of fulfillment in the other three areas will bring contentment or sufficient meaning to life. We can be certain of this: *Harmony with God is essential and must be sought first.* "Seek first his kingdom and his righteousness, and all these things will be given to you as well" (Matt. 6:33).

Only when we have a relationship to Christ do we find the wisdom and power to bring our lives into effective balance. Christ said, "I have come that they [which includes you and me] may have life, and have it to the full" (John 10:10b). This means that even though life has its troubles, we can have a fair share of joys and delights. Even though we have rough edges in our lives, God can reshape, sand, and polish us into smoothness. Even though we may face loneliness in our lives, we can have friendship and companionship with the Son of God.

Most of us—maybe all of us—start our quest for fulfillment with relationship with God because it works. That's an adequate reason, but a better reason is because God is worthy. The best reason is because we love God. Because of our love for him, we respond to him with living patterns that flow out of natural obedience.

When we bring God into our heart, we reap three rewards. First, a relationship to God reduces the number and severity of the difficult situations we create as we pursue fulfillment in the other three areas. Second, with God in our heart, we have the comfort and support of the Holy Spirit. Third, God guides us and enables us to deal with reversals and adversities in the difficult situations we experience.

DOING AND BEING

The world says that if we have physical security and comfort, receive cooperation and adulation from other people, and have the money and freedom to do things we enjoy doing, we will be happy. Maybe we will. But Christianity says happiness is not enough.

Christianity points out the limitations of happiness and advises us to pursue life so we gain contentment. Although people who aren't reconciled to God can find short-term happiness from the environment, others, and self, contentment comes only when we have first found peace with God.

The world finds happiness in *doing*. Think of bumper stickers: "Happiness is a sailboat." "I'd rather be sky diving." "I ♥ bowling."

The Bible tells us that we can find happiness in *being*. "Happy are those whose sins are forgiven, whose wrongs are pardoned. Happy is the man . . . who is free from all deceit'' (Ps. 32:1–2 TEV). "Happy are those who trust the LORD " (Ps. 40:4a TEV). "Happy are those who are concerned for the poor'' (Ps. 41:1a TEV).

Wendy Williams, Olympic medalist in 10-meter platform diving, found she became stale and ineffective at one point, so she took six months off to work, visit friends, and travel. To use the vocabulary of this book, she took time away from her doing (diving) to gain perspective on her being (what life means to her). Having done that, she found much greater success when she returned to the "doing" of diving. This is a valid and important redirection of emphasis.

We can never find happiness or peace in relationship with God by doing, no matter how righteous the ends of our doing may be. No amount of doing can satisfy our need for being. When we are slaves to the activities of our doing, we are positioned with our backs to God—away from the position of developing in relationship with God—which is the cornerstone of our being. If our doing reduces effectiveness in living, it's wrong.

ONE KIND OF PERFECTION TO SEEK

There is one area of life in which we should try to be perfect—in our intention to know and please God. We know that our behavior can never be perfect, but our desire for perfect love can be total. When we give ourselves completely to God, our relationship to him will change. As a result, our thoughts, attitudes, and behavior also will change.

Although our commitment to God is the one point in life at which we should strive for perfection, it's often the point at which we are most complacent. Perhaps because commitment is intangible, we are less aware it; because it's hidden from others, we don't get praised for it; because we can't measure it, we can fool ourselves about its strength. Or we may substitute quantity of doing for quality of intention.

JESUS: PERFECT, NOT A PERFECTIONIST

Although Jesus was perfect, he was not a perfectionist. For example, when he was faced with overwhelming demands, Jesus didn't meet every need. On several occasions he left places without doing all the teaching and healing the people wanted from him. Instead, he went away for rest and renewal, or he went to teach in other places or he took time to be alone with his disciples (Matt. 8:16–18; Mark 1:37–38; Luke 5:15–16; John 11:54). Most perfectionists would be overwhelmed and indecisive when faced with these multiple demands.

Jesus was not pressured by time as was his friend Martha, a task-oriented compulsive who was unhappy because Jesus, even though he had known her brother was sick, had waited two days before coming to see them. Martha said to Jesus, "If you had been here, my brother would not have died" (John 11:21). Jesus had his good reasons for the delay, but he was in control. He later raised Lazarus from the dead. Perfectionists worry about time and the future. Jesus said, "Do not worry about tomorrow" (Matt. 6:34a).

Perfectionists perform to get attention; Jesus did not seek fame (Luke 8:56), although it came to him (Matt. 9:26). Perfectionists have difficulty delegating (they think no one else can do it well enough), but Jesus actively delegated his work: first he chose twelve disciples and sent them on a mission (Matt. 9:36–11:1); later he sent seventy more disciples on a mission (Luke 10:1–24); and he prepared the way for a new order in which the kingdom work is at the hands of each of us.

THE HARMONIZING HEART

Chapter 5 introduced the diagnostic diamond, a tool for analyzing problems and finding their causes. In that pattern, God's design for living (*D* in I–D–E–A–S) was placed outside the heart to emphasize that God's truth is an entity that exists apart from our humanness, represented by the heart.

The gist of Christianity, however, is that through our decision to accept God's offer of reconciliation, we bring God's design into our heart. That is the condition of the *harmonizing heart,* illustrated in figure 6.[1]

Figure 6

THE HARMONIZING HEART

Note that God's presence pervades every area of the heart, represented by the *Y* for Yahweh, the Hebrew equivalent to the name Jehovah. The heart is filled with and organized around the presence of Yahweh, the one God. His presence touches every intellection/decision, emotion, and action. This power fills our heart when we accept God's offer of reconciliation with him, made possible by the life, death, and resurrection of his son, Jesus Christ.

The harmonizing heart is still in the midst of situations (the *S*'s surrounding the heart)—large and small, good and bad, painful and pleasant, sizzling or soothing.

Some situations are thrust on us without our choice; others are consequences of our actions. Accepting God's design strengthens Christians in two ways: they are protected against the attack of hostile situations, and they generate fewer harmful consequences.

THE DIVIDING HEART

However, when we refuse to bring God's design into our heart or if we push it aside in disobedience, our heart becomes a *dividing heart,* illustrated in figure 7. The heart is fragmented with no harmonizing element to integrate the intellection/decisions with the emotions or actions. The dividing heart can't remain intact when it is assaulted by the difficult situations (S) around it. Ignoring or refusing God's design weakens people in two ways: they have less capacity to deal with difficult situations, and they create more difficult situations.

Figure 7

THE DIVIDING HEART

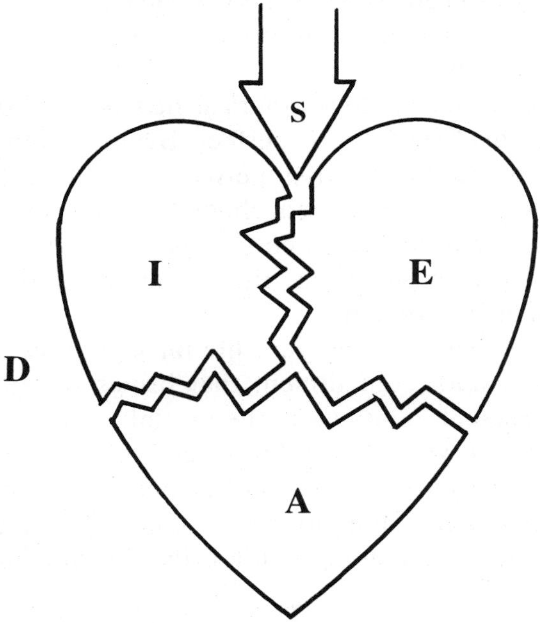

Don't scold yourself for being an imperfect human being. God doesn't. God meets and loves you where you are. He knows you can't be perfect, so he doesn't expect you to be. His love for you frees you to love yourself and to have a relationship to him. Go ahead, love yourself and say, "Here I come, God, perfect or not."

But we must be careful not to take a cavalier or half-hearted attitude toward God's authority, to casually dismiss or ignore his designs and indulge in our own pleasures. Competing with God's design for living is foolishness and pride. Using our imperfection as an excuse to cut corners in our moral behavior is also foolish. To safeguard against these foolish urges, we must have regular fellowship with God, admitting our sins and asking him to show us sins we don't see. Can you pray, asking God to help you see your sin as he sees it and to help you become uncomfortable with your sin? That's a gutsy prayer.

Pride may also be the root of harsh and condemning attitudes toward self. When we condemn ourselves, we are seeking to usurp God's authority and this, too, is foolishness and pride.

Christ asks us to love others as he has loved us, a tall order, since his love for us is perfect. Begin with the desire and intention to love Christ perfectly—with everything you are and have—and then choose to love others that way. Seek perfection of intention, not performance; the more perfect your intention, the closer the performance will approach perfection.

Change will occur in your life through three actions: first, make a faith commitment that brings reconciliation with God; second, continue in the disciplines of study and prayer through which you know and experience God; third, grow in your intention to obey perfectly. Until your being is rooted in intent to please God, your efforts to change thinking and doing can't bring satisfaction.

APPLICATION

1. Pray the "gutsy prayer," asking God to show you your sins and the parts of your life you aren't willing to have him enter. If you can't pray that, ask God to prepare you to pray it.

2. Consider how you use your time. How much time do you spend in Bible study, prayer, and quietness with the Lord compared to the amounts wasted or given to foolishness? Being comes before doing, remember. But our doing is an accurate measure of what is important to us. Looking at your use of time may show you that your intentions aren't what you think they are.

3. Think thoughtfully and creatively about a regular time for strengthening your relationship with God through study, prayer, and listening. Make a plan and then use it.

9

Change What You Think

One of the most important foundation stones upon which the structure of this book is built comes from Romans 12:2, "Do not conform any longer to the pattern of this world, but be transformed by the renewing of your mind." The verse describes a principle for living, and this chapter offers methods that are consistent with the principle.

It's much easier for me to suggest a technique than it will be for you to use the technique. We both know that. I wish I could change that part, but I can't. I can tell you this, though: I have seen many people find tremendous changes in their lives by using processes described in this chapter.

I hope that as you have been reading this book you have been asking God to help you find and use the information that you need. Please be joyous in praising God for his majesty, humble in thanking him for his mercy, and bold in asking for his help. The time you spend communicating with God about your problem of perfectionism is the most important, productive time that you invest into the matter.

Some of the methods in this chapter are based on the principle of *displacement,* which is a practical application of Romans 12:21, which says, "Do not be overcome by evil, but overcome evil with good." Displacing evil— pushing it out by bringing in good—is one way to overcome evil with good. You can't just kick out the bad, for that leaves a vacuum for something else, perhaps equally undesirable, to rush in—a hazard Jesus described in Matthew 12:43–45. Displacement pushes out the unwanted by bringing in the desired.

Some of the other techniques in this chapter are based on the assumption that it's appropriate for us to think well of ourselves. This is not the same as pride but simply is enthusiasm for being created in God's image and having kinship with God. Perfectionists need to displace their disparaging thoughts about themselves with the factual affirmation of worth. As believers we are God's special property—we are *worthwhile!*

Keep in mind, then, that the methods described in this chapter are ways to put the biblical principle into practice. And remember that we can't change on our own strength.

APPLICATION

1. **Ask God to teach you what you need to learn about your perfectionism (or about the perfectionist you live near).** Ask him to help you be aware of harmful attitudes such as resentment, bogus beliefs, and shackles of fear or pride that would interfere with changing your mental patterns and outlook on life.

2. **Identify your bogus beliefs.** Chapter 3 encouraged you to begin listening to the bogus beliefs within your mind. If you have been doing that, you're already on your way to breaking out of the perfectionism trap. If you haven't done this yet, go back to the application section of chapter 3 and follow the instructions there.

3. **Learn the truth.** Learn what views can replace your bogus views. Study the examples in table 6 to help you devise true views that can replace your own bogus beliefs. Respond to the bogus beliefs expressed in statements 9–11 by writing in a true view.

Table 6
BOGUS BELIEFS AND TRUE VIEWS

Bogus Belief	True View
1. If my work isn't perfect, I'm no good.	1. I'm valuable because God loves me. That's enough.
2. Other people are better than I am because they perform better.	2. We're all valuable. I don't need to make comparisons.
3. I am not doing well enough.	3. I'm careful to do my best and that's the right amount.
4. I have never done well enough.	4. I'm doing my best in this moment and looking forward to the future.
5. If I'm not perfect, no one will like me.	5. My friendships are not based on performance.
6. Being perfect isn't just a good thing, it's the *only* thing.	6. I get great satisfaction from doing the best I can do.
7. It's possible to be perfect, and I better be!	7. It's not possible to be perfect; I choose to pursue excellence.
8. Performance equals worth.	8. Worth is a gift from God; I'm worthwhile because he loves me.
9. I could never do anything well enough for him.	9.
10. If only I could make All-State, maybe he	10.

would pat me on the
back.

11. If I keep up the good   11.
    work, it will be all right,
    but if I don't, it will be
    awful.

4. **Write out some of your bogus beliefs and the true views that contradict those beliefs.** Continue this activity for several days so that you can gather a full list of your faulty thinking patterns.

5. **Give yourself permission to learn from other people.** Greg Louganis, four-time Olympic gold medalist and five-time world diving champion said, "There is so much I can learn from watching other competitors." This young man, described often as the greatest diver of all time, gives us a good illustration of teachability.

6. **Carry out a popularity campaign about yourself with yourself.** Get a pad of "Post-it" self-adhesive memos. On one of the sheets, write a sentence affirming yourself. For example:

I like [insert your name] because _____
_____.

I respect [insert your name] because _____
_____.

[insert your name] is okay because _____
_____.

Stick this memo to a surface where you will see it easily. Write another one tomorrow and put that in a visible place in a different room. Add one each day for two weeks. Don't take any of them down until you have posted at least fourteen affirmations about yourself. If you have a roommate or family, they can do this too—for themselves and for one another. Leave the notes up if visitors come so they can share your enthusiasm for being you. (I think it will probably inspire them to think more charitably and beneficially toward themselves too.)

7. **Stop bogus beliefs that repeat themselves in your mind.** If you have a bogus belief that pops into your mind ten or more times a day, the thought-stopping technique will be useful. Here is how to do it. When the unwanted thought comes into your mind, say "Stop!" If conditions allow, say this out loud. If other people are around, just shout "Stop!" vividly in your mind. Immediately displace the unwanted thought with a nourishing thought. For example:

   • Pray in thanksgiving or praise.
   • Pray for the welfare of another person.
   • Sing or hum a hymn.
   • Say or read a poem or Scripture verse.
   • List some of your blessings.

It will also work if you bring in a neutral thought. For example, recite the alphabet or recite the alphabet backward or simply count for a few seconds. While these latter activities won't nourish you, at least they won't be destructive like the bogus belief.

8. **Keep perspective.** If you are angry or having a pity party, look yourself eye to eye in a mirror and talk out loud about what's going on. This will help you get things back in perspective. You may even laugh at the way you're exaggerating the facts. Writing a letter to yourself about it or just writing out a few thoughts can break the grip of the bogus belief.

9. **Make posters that express true views to displace your bogus beliefs.** The posters don't have to be fancy; neatness doesn't count. This activity will help you because you are consciously discarding the bogus belief and affirming the facts.

10. **Give yourself permission to be less than perfect.** Call yourself by name, out loud, and say, "You have my permission to be less than perfect when you [mention the next activity]."

11. **If you are changing a habit, remind yourself to do things the new way.** Buy some small, round stickers in your favorite color and stick a few around your part of the world to prompt you to think the new way. Then, when you see the sticker, remember to think, "[Your name], you're doing your best and that is just wonderful!" These will remind you of whatever you want them to remind you of: to affirm yourself or others, to pray for yourself or others, to count your blessings and be thankful, or whatever. It's not a ritual that is important because it is doing; it is a way to change your way of being.

12. **Talk over your situation with God.** Are you in pain because of anger toward those who taught you harmful ways of thinking, from the hurt of traumatic events (recent or from decades ago), or because you are convinced that it will never be possible for you to get rid of habits that limit your freedom? Don't hesitate to describe your needs and desires to God, asking him to direct you to the understanding and assistance you need.

13. **Talk over your situation with other Christians.** Sometimes it can be difficult to talk to God about your situation. Some of you who read this are angry with God because your experience with an earthly father was so unpleasant or because you didn't have that experience at all. For others it's difficult because God is distant and hard to comprehend. If it's difficult to approach God directly, get acquainted with some of his people. Find a church that offers teaching from the Bible, worship that you find meaningful, and fellow-

ship with godly people. Consider talking with a pastor or a Christian counselor about your needs and inquire how God can become more personal in your life.

10

Change What You Do

I hope that by the time you read this chapter, you have found your bogus beliefs and are displacing them with true views. Changing the way you think puts you well on your way toward living more completely by God's design, which will bring you greater contentment.

Now let's consider how your actions can change. This chapter describes not only strategies to evaluate the contentment you get from what you do but also strategies to change disruptive actions.

ACTIONS FOLLOW THOUGHTS

All of us think before we act. When things happen quickly, it may not seem as if we have time to think, but we do. Sometimes we hear people say, "I just did that without thinking." They really did think, but they did it so quickly that they weren't consciously aware of their thought processes.

Some actions we take without thinking are called habits. Habits can be helpful or harmful. Many habits improve life and make a person more pleasant to be around: looking carefully when driving toward an intersection, jogging, attending church regularly, saying thank you after receiving courtesy. Other habits erode the quality of life: excessive TV watching, overeating, griping, talking sarcastically about people.

Some habits happen reflexively (e.g., covering the mouth when sneezing, shouting joyously upon hearing good news). Other habits are patterns of lifestyle, part of the weekly routine (e.g., having a Big Mac for lunch every Saturday, watching a particular TV show on Monday nights). Many habits fall somewhere between the reflexive ones and the routine ones (e.g., parking the car away from other cars in a parking lot so it won't get bumped, clearing the dirty dishes off the table at the end of a meal).

HABITS COMMON AMONG PERFECTIONISTS

Several types of harmful habits are often found among perfectionists.

1. Bogus beliefs that produce destructive mental habits. For instance, perfectionists who believe they are worthless get into the destructive habit of berating themselves when they have performed less than perfectly.

2. Compulsive behavior. Perfectionists often get into habits that involve excessive checking to see that everything is just right (e.g., that the doors are locked at night, adding the checkbook balance five times, measuring the ingredients for a batch of cookies several times). Among Christians this may find expression in repeated confession of sins with petition for forgiveness (which of course was given at the point of original repentance).

3. Rituals to ward off danger or make good things happen. The folklore of children has long included bogus advice claiming magical power such as, "Step on a crack, break your mother's back." Major-league sports are rampant with superstitions among players and coaches— the lucky baseball cap or a particular sequence for putting on the uniform. Because perfectionists value performance so highly, exaggerate the consequences of failure so much, and live in such dread of failure, they are vulnerable to adopting ridiculous rituals.

4. Excessive attention to detail or social propriety. I recall an electrician who, in wiring new houses, measured to find the center of the studs before drilling holes to put the wires through. This added nothing to the quality of the job. What seemed to him to be meritorious attention to detail was wasteful and foolish.

Because actions like these limit the person's freedom, we might call them "handcuff habits." What handcuff habits lower the quality of your life? Whatever they are, you can find them and change them.

ACTIONS INFLUENCE THOUGHTS

I have said several times that we think before we act; therefore changing what we think changes what we do. But the dynamic works in the other direction too. What we do also influences what we think. This influence can be for better or worse. If we think we can do a task but we don't do it, our action (of not doing it) forces us to believe that maybe we couldn't do it. Now we have two beliefs about that task, and the two beliefs are in conflict with each other. That's harmful. On the other hand, if we thought we couldn't do the task but we did it anyway, our action would demonstrate that we could do the task, displacing the belief that we couldn't. The result is absence of conflict and more confidence—both great improvements. The influence of our *actions* can be strong enough to turn our *thinking* away from bogus beliefs that support handcuff habits and toward true views.

The next section explains more about the relationship between thinking and doing and then describes methods to help you change what you do.

Handcuff habits grow out of the assumption that being perfect is necessary. You have rejected that assumption, and now it's time to reject the harmful behavior that came from it. You can do that. If habits are learned, then they also can be unlearned. These methods will help you do it.

1. Choose actions on the basis of your goals, not on the basis of feelings. Decide to do those things that advance your goals and do them whether or not you feel like it. Reject the bogus belief that says you can do only what you feel like doing.

2. Bring balance into your life. Have you lost the balance between production and leisure? If so, even it up. When leisure is in proportion to production, it brings necessary renewal so production can continue. Adequate leisure is not laziness, it's a responsibility.

3. Assertively resist undue pressures from other people. If you find that you say yes when you want to say no, learn to say no. Even the Christian needs to say no, just as Jesus did. Look at the big picture so you know when to say no, improve your skills in saying no, then be assertive on behalf of what is valuable in the long run.

4. Evaluate your use of time. During some hours of the week, you are free to do whatever you would like to do. Have you considered giving a tenth of this time in activities that are for the benefit of other people? Great satisfaction and emotional energy come from sharing. Check your use of time to see the proportions between time spent just for yourself and time invested into the betterment of others.

5. When you identify a handcuff habit, break its control by deliberately sloughing off or failing. It worked that way for several people I know.

Priscilla had a handcuff habit of daily vacuuming the rugs in her house. She knew it was absurd to do this, but she wasn't able to talk herself out of it. In response to my challenge, she broke out of those handcuffs this way: She dumped the grubby contents of her kitchen wastebasket onto the center of her living-room carpet and let the trash stay there for a week. It was a relief to her and her husband when she cleaned up the mess, but she had broken the handcuffs and found new freedom. From that point on,

Priscilla didn't vacuum the carpets unless they needed it, which she happily discovered to be weekly or less often.

Priscilla defied her handcuff habit of excessive vacuuming with a vivid symbol—trash in the living room. This new behavior was temporary. Although the gesture was symbolic, it needed to be more than a half-hearted, token expression and couldn't be destructive to other people. Priscilla talked with her husband before she dumped the kitchen trash, and of course she looked through the trash to make sure it contained nothing that would permanently damage the carpet.

Quentin wore a three-piece suit and tie almost all the time. He was such a fussy dresser that it made other people uncomfortable. Dressing this way was a nuisance to him too. For example, if he was fixing something in the basement of his house and needed to go buy materials, he would get out of his blue jeans and T-shirt and put on dressy slacks and a fancy shirt to go to the lumber yard.

It was very hard for Quentin to defy his handcuff habit but he did. When he went to the church picnic, he wore faded blue jeans and a sweatshirt. He blended in beautifully with the rest of the men and discovered that he had more freedom to enjoy the picnic because he wasn't worried about damaging good clothing.

Riley was handcuffed by being willing to go to church only if his car was sparkling clean inside and out. On more than one occasion he had washed his car by hand in his driveway at 11:30 Saturday night after driving long hours on the way home from vacation. Finally he chose to break out of those handcuffs by driving to church with his car caked with dust. He blended in as well as Quentin had, and Riley found it liberating.

I don't for a moment disparage cleanliness, neatness, or other virtues; I value them. But when allegiance to a virtue unbalances a person's life, then that virtue has become an enemy, not an ally.

6. Identify actions that bring satisfaction. The diagnostic diamond already may have helped you identify some of these actions, but here's another way to analyze your activities. Make a chart like the one in table 7.[1] List your activities on the left side and fill in your responses to each of the categories. Then compare the level of satisfaction with the level of effectiveness. You may find that you get great satisfaction from activities you don't do particularly well and little satisfaction from others you do effectively. This may suggest that perfect performance isn't the most important objective. Then use the diagnostic diamond to examine the I–D–E–A–S that surround some of these activities. Use all of this information to help you see what changes need to be made in your life.

Table 7

SATISFACTION ANALYSIS

Record satisfaction and effectiveness on a scale of 0% (no satisfaction) to 100% (maximum satisfaction).

Activity	Predict How Satisfying the Activity Will Be	Record How Satisfying It Actually Was	Record How Effectively You Performed
	20%	75%	99%
Set up chairs for church banquet	Analysis: I met some new people, which was fun, and it felt good to "help the cause" at church.		
	80%	80%/20%	99%
Watch TV all evening	Analysis: The enjoyment tapered off rapidly as I moved from leisure to laziness.		
	80%	80%	40%/90%
Bowling with church team	Analysis: I had an off night bowling (40%), but our team is in it for fun; great fellowship (90%).		
	90%	100%	30%
Fix bicycle	Analysis: I expected this to be simple, but what frustration! It took three trips to		

get parts and tools, but I got the job done. Whoopee!

10%	65%	50%

Teach Sunday school to fourth graders

Analysis: If I do this more (maybe I will), I'd like to learn how to teach. I expected to flop, but the kids were responsive. I was scared but happy. Next time, I'll look forward to it more.

20%	90%	90%

Study manual for my job

Analysis: This part of my job is drudgery but has to be done. I'm pleased with my self-discipline in getting this chore out of the way.

7. Everything you do should be beneficial to you. Sometimes the benefit is in the *process* of doing. For example, you read a novel and find you enjoy the process of reading. In other situations the benefit may be in the *outcome*. For example, when you read a technical manual for your job, the process of reading is laborious, but you benefit from the outcome—greater competence on the job. Think about things you do and find the benefits in both the processes and outcomes.

8. Refuse to be controlled by fear. If some of your actions bring you fear, you can respond to those actions in four ways: first, don't do them and then scold yourself for not doing them; second, don't do them but give yourself permission not to do them; third, do them in spite of the fear; and fourth, get rid of the fear. If the activities are rewarding to you, then reject the first and second options.

But how do you get rid of fear? Start by working out a diagnostic diamond, tracing backward in time to see what you can learn about where your fear began. I'm certain that you'll find some bogus beliefs. You may also find some old traumas that continue to hang over you like dark clouds, rumbling and threatening, making you think there may be another storm.

Defy the fear in a way similar to defying handcuff

habits. Do the thing you fear. In most cases you'll find that this breaks up the cloud and lets the sun shine where the shadow of the cloud has been. I encourage you to consider talking with a wise friend, pastor, or Christian counselor about your fears if they're keeping you from doing things you want to do or if you're condemning yourself for having them. On the other hand, everyone is afraid of various things, so don't expect to be totally without fear.

9. Know when to give up. Mark Twain once said, "Don't try to teach a pig to sing. It's a waste of time and annoys the pig."

11

Procrastination:
Change It Without Putting It Off

Perfectionists do two things almost perfectly: criticize themselves and procrastinate. Procrastination (putting off doing something until later) is a cousin to perfectionism. The family trait they have in common is fear of failure coupled with the belief that if they fail, they'll be criticized and rejected.

THE COSTS OF PROCRASTINATION

Procrastination is expensive. Procrastination has emotional costs: anxiety, irritability (which always accompanies anxiety), and eventually feelings of despair and depression. Procrastination also has situational costs. Put off returning a phone call and you may miss an invitation to a party. Delay checking the oil in your car engine and you may have an expensive repair. Postpone having a physical examination and your body may develop a life-threatening condition. Delay making a commitment of faith in Christ and miss eternal happiness. Delay knowing the Lord personally and reduce contentment in this life.

WHY PERFECTIONISM LEADS TO
PROCRASTINATION

For perfectionists, life is like going through a revolving door while they are wearing skis. When they look at their "to do" lists, they see one impossible expectation after another. When frustration is just around the corner, it makes sense to put things off until later; it makes sense to skip the tasks that look like failures and do the easier things, whether or not they are important. Wouldn't you rather tackle a job at which you are guaranteed success than one in which you are guaranteed to fail? Of course! Tomorrow is soon enough to fail.

Procrastination is a quick fix for the anxiety of impending failure. How helpful have quick fixes been for you?

The goal of perfectionists is to be in control, but since perfection is impossible, perfectionists are never in control. If they can't control how well they do something, they can at least control what they do. This makes many perfectionists quite eager to tackle new projects, hoping that at last they'll be satisfied with their performance. As soon as perfectionists see that the latest project will be no more perfect than the others, they find it hard to stay with it; then they start looking again for new projects. Switching from something productive to something trivial provides at least the illusion of being in control.

Perfectionists contend with a lot of frustration, and frustration breeds anger. One way to express anger toward another person is not to do something that person would like done. This attack by being inactive is called passive aggression and often can be the motivating force behind some procrastination.

Although not all procrastinators are perfectionists, most perfectionists are strongly tempted to procrastinate. Often. If you want to change that in your own life, you can.

What can you do about procrastination? Reading this book puts you well on your way toward change because resolving the causes of perfectionism very often resolves the causes of procrastination. But that can take some time. While you're working on the long-term solution, you can also use the following techniques to help you temporarily manage your procrastination.

1. Know the costs. What does your procrastination cost you? Write down at least five examples of the cost you have paid for procrastinating.

2. Appetizer tasks. Fine meals often begin with hors d'oeuvres, tasty morsels to stimulate your appetite for the food that will follow. You can do the same thing with many of your large tasks. Identify those pieces that are especially attractive to you—the most appetizing. Do those first and then transition into the "main course."

3. Do the worst first. Maybe you're the kind of person who needs to do the worst first rather than the most appetizing first. Try this method. Identify the most disagreeable chore (project, job, task) you need to do. Then do it. Getting the ugliest item off your list makes the whole list look more attractive, and you'll feel good after you have finished.

4. Reward yourself. When you have made some measurable progress, give yourself a special, enjoyable reward. Make a list of ways you could reward yourself— watch TV, eat ice cream, take a nap, go shopping, play tennis, get your hair styled. Then when you have completed a task you ordinarily would have put off, reward yourself. You have earned it.

5. Chop the job. Cut the big job into a lot of smaller jobs. This not only makes it easier to start the job, but it also gives you the satisfaction of completing many small jobs instead of waiting to finish a large job. For example, if you procrastinate about doing your income tax, sort the receipts on the first evening, tally up your charitable contributions the next, and so on. Then choose one large task and break it into smaller parts. Complete it one piece at a time.

6. Take a single step. A Chinese proverb says, "A journey of a thousand miles begins with a single step." Think about that, recognizing the value in getting started, no matter how little you may do at the beginning. If you do a little at a time, eventually a very large project will be finished. I can only write sentences, not books. But if I put together enough well-organized sentences, I may have a book. Which of your tasks seems like a thousand-mile journey? Identify the small single step that you *can* take on that journey and do it.

7. Set a deadline. Procrastination is often a problem of not having a defined time space in which to do a task. Your task list will be stronger if you put deadlines on the items. Look at your own list and put deadlines on the three most important items on your list.

8. Now won. No, that's not the name of an oriental soup; it's something you can say to celebrate when you do a task as soon as it needs to be done. There is a close connection between when you do the work—now—and the outcome—won. Turn n–o–w around and you have w–o–n; turn your habit of procrastination around and you will have w–o–n! Put up a card with the words *NOW WON* where you see it during the times you are likely to procrastinate. Let it be a gentle reminder that doing it *now* is good for you.

9. Go on record. Hold yourself accountable by telling someone what commitment you have made to yourself about a project. Ask that person to hold you accountable for the three deadlines you added to your to do list.

10. Glue time together. Time is an elusive, intangible commodity, but it can be glued together. Now that you have figured out how to break a large job into small pieces, you can use small pieces of time to do the small tasks. In effect, this "glues" the small fragments of time together by unifying them around the large task. Break one of the tasks on your list into smaller bits. Each time you do a bit of work on that task, record the number of minutes. Six short segments of time—5 minutes, 7 minutes, 10 minutes, 5 minutes, 5 minutes, and 8 minutes—add up to 40 minutes, which is enough to bring a sense of accomplishment on many projects.

11. The five-minute jail sentence. If you had been imprisoned in solitary confinement during the last two weeks, you probably would leap at a chance to do the most unpleasant task on your list. Okay, you can still leap at it if you want to; it's the same task. Why let it seem so horrible just because you have been having fun for two weeks? Choose one task that you have been putting off and don't let yourself do anything else until you have worked on the task for five minutes.

RESOLVING PROCRASTINATION

These techniques are a good start on dealing with procrastination, but they aren't enough. They will only temporarily reduce the pain of procrastination. You must also resolve the fundamental problems.

Most procrastination will clear up when perfectionism is resolved. If you have used the diagnostic diamond to analyze your circumstances, you probably have found procrastination in your I–D–E–A–S sequences and understand why it is taken care of when the root causes are remedied. I encourage you to give careful attention to that.

Some people use procrastination as a way of attacking others. "Nice people" choose passive-aggressive methods because they disapprove of direct methods of attack. For this reason, they need outside help to discover the true nature of their behavior. This help can come from a wise friend, a professional counselor, and through the instruction of the Holy Spirit.

If you suspect that you have procrastinated as a way of attacking someone else, ask God to teach you what you need to learn about yourself. Pray that you will become aware of every need to confess and repent, to make amends with others, and to develop better human relations.

Pray, too, for clarity about what's important to do. Not everything on your list is of equal importance. The world's priorities are much different from God's design, and it's hard for us to keep our thinking from being contaminated by world thinking. Carefully, prayerfully evaluate your priorities. You will procrastinate less when you have confidence that you are putting your efforts into activities that really matter.

12

Workaholism:
Change It Without Working at It

Workaholism—the condition of working so much that spiritual life, health, interpersonal relationships, or contentment are diminished—is a sin people get praised for. It's idolatry to give work greater importance than relationship with God. We disregard his design if we give more attention to our work than to our families.

WHY PEOPLE WORK

God created us with the desire to work. Work provides what we need for physical survival. Work fulfills our need for identity and helps us express our creativity. It's right for us to want to work industriously. However, the workaholic overdoes it—and pays a price.

We find meaning in work in several ways. Observe five people working with single-minded discipline and detail:

Twelve-year-old Shana practices figure skating twenty-two hours a week. She hopes to skate in the Olympics in a few years and then in one of the major ice shows. She finds practice laborious and sometimes boring, but she doesn't mind. She says, "Someday I'll hear the applause, and it will be worth all the hard work I'm doing now."

Troy sands the fender of an antique auto he's restoring to better-than-new condition. He's absorbed in what he's doing and couldn't be dragged away to do anything else. He says that when the car is finished, it will be too nice to drive and too precious to sell. Impractical? "No way," Troy says, "I'm having the time of my life!"

Ursula, a concert violinist, practices diligently to learn an intricate violin concerto. She thinks often of the embarrassment of missing a note during a concert or of getting bad reviews. She is as tense as the strings on her instrument, but she continues to drive herself relentlessly. "If I don't," she says, "I could have a bad performance and discredit myself for life."

Vance studies corporate financial reports hour after hour, looking for information other investors have over- looked and plotting strategies to exploit the stock market. He candidly admits, "I hate my job, but as long as my clients pay me as lavishly as they do for my advice, I'll keep doing it. It buys me the good life."

Wendall is almost always in his laboratory at the chemical company where he works. His wife says, "He comes home to sleep and that's about it." Wendall defends his long hours by describing the pressure he feels to finish developing a new product. He say that if he isn't finished soon, he'll be fired. He has been saying that for twenty years. The fact is, Wendall stays at the lab because he doesn't want to go home.

Five people working diligently—five different rea- sons. Shana works for a future reward. Troy is rewarded immediately from the work itself. Vance doesn't like his work, but he exchanges the money he earns for trips and entertainment. Ursula is motivated by fear. Wendall works because he is uncomfortable at home.

Are they all workaholics? Not necessarily. Probably just Ursula.

The workaholic *must* work; the well-adjusted person *wants* to work. There is a world of difference in the motivation of a person who is compelled by a mega-voice shouting "you should" and another who is finding expression of abilities and interests in work. You can't tell them apart by looking.

WHY PERFECTIONISM LEADS TO WORKAHOLISM

Not all workaholics are perfectionists. Most workaholics are motivated by greed for money, fame, or power—not by the desire to perform perfectly. Their distortion is of quantity, not of quality.

But many perfectionists are workaholics. Striving for the impossible, they have to be. The impossible isn't achieved easily, is it?

Another reason perfectionists overwork is because they want to please others. They are pushovers for more work and suckers for taking on additional tasks. And in the hope of finally finding an activity they can do perfectly, some of them jump from activity to activity.

Perfectionists also need to please themselves. Their consciences will not allow them to give up. They work harder and harder, not out of joy in the activities themselves or with satisfaction in the attainment of excellence, but out of fear of rejection or another kind of failure.

Perfectionists seek the praise of someone important. Yet the force that motivates perfectionists is often criticism from that same person.

THE COSTS OF WORKAHOLISM

The workaholic is usually too busy to notice the problem for what it is until the costs have become quite expensive. The costs of workaholism include:

- Disruption of family life.
- Neglect of spiritual growth and fellowship.
- Diminishing returns from effort. The Pennsylvania Dutch have a saying: "The hurrier I go the

behinder I get." That's the condition of the workaholic trying to get caught up, and it breeds more frustration.

- Physical tension—neglect of rest, exercise, relaxation, and recreation that help ward off health problems.
- Loss of perspective about the larger issues of vocation or even about life. The workaholic develops tunnel vision with an ever-decreasing field of view.
- Misdirected resentment. Workaholics are likely to feel angry about the pain associated with their efforts and sacrifices. Although their dilemma is the result of a long series of personal choices, they are likely to blame someone else, further disrupting their own life.

MANAGING WORKAHOLISM

Don't try to justify these costs or let them continue. Instead, resolve the fundamental problem. For the perfectionistic workaholic, resolving the causes of perfectionism will probably eliminate the causes of workaholism. While you are working on that long-term solution, use these techniques to help you manage your inclination toward workaholism.

1. Understand what motivates you to work. Answer these questions: Why do I work? To earn reward? If so, is the reward present or future? Are the rewards only of this world (e.g., fame) or are eternal values primary (e.g., improving the condition of other people)? Do the rewards come from the activities or from the money? Am I motivated by fear? If so, what produces that fear? Is work a place to hide? From what? Discuss these matters with a wise family member or friend.

2. Set limits. Decide in advance how long you will work, write the time down, and when it's time to quit, quit.

3. Be accountable. When you take the pledge to

swear off work, tell people. Then let them pull you away from the work when the time comes.

4. Schedule balance into your life. Put recreation, Bible study, and prayer—or whatever you are neglecting—into your schedule. Don't let yourself skip any of these activities, just as you wouldn't let yourself miss a job-related meeting.

RESOLVING WORKAHOLISM

The chapter title says, "Change it without working at it." Is that possible? You certainly can't change workaholism with panicky, compulsive efforts. But changing also doesn't happen automatically.

1. You need to choose. Breaking your addiction to work begins with a choice. One option is to pursue the world's values. Like pleasure—the world says, "Go for the gusto." Or money—the world defines the Golden Rule as "He who has the gold, rules." Or power—when John F. Kennedy was asked why he wanted to become president, he replied, "Because that's where the power is."

The other option is to live by God's design. We are called to living, not just to making a living. God's design has priorities—God, family, work—giving attention to each in proper proportion. It sometimes seems like a more complicated way to live than the single-minded pursuit of a world value such as money or fame. But it isn't, and it brings durable contentment that the world can't bring.

Our choice is the same one Joshua delivered to the tribes of Israel: "But if serving the Lord seems undesirable to you, then choose for yourselves this day whom you will serve, whether the gods your forefathers served beyond the River, or the gods of the Amorites, in whose land you are living." I hope that you will respond with Joshua: "But as for me and my household, we will serve the Lord" (Josh. 24:15).

2. Learn what motivates your workaholism. Review the ideas in this chapter and pray for God's help in finding the answers for your life. If you discover that you are working excessively to escape a difficult situation or relationship, seek counseling for healing and improvement in those circumstances.

3. Examine your beliefs. Make sure the teaching you receive is biblical and balanced. Talk with your pastor or primary spiritual mentor about the issue of works and grace. Then pray, seeking to know if you are fully enjoying God's abundant grace or are pridefully diminishing it by acting as if you must earn your salvation.

4. Deal with perfectionism before workaholism. If you think you are both a perfectionist and a workaholic, forget about the workaholism for the present. Concentrate on changing the beliefs, habits, and relationships that undergird your perfectionism. As you work on your perfectionism, your work habits most likely will fall into place.

13

How to Live with a Perfectionist

Perfectionists—people who take such great pains that they give them to others; people who have one toothbrush for the upper teeth and another for the lower; the guy who uses the eraser end of the pencil more than the point and the bride who, when she swept down the aisle, swept down the aisle!

If you live with a perfectionist, you know how difficult it can be. When perfectionists expect the impossible from themselves, frustration ripples to touch all the people around them. Their exacting requirements can be as much fun to live with as the sound of fingernails on a blackboard.

If you have had to walk on eggshells while living with a perfectionist, this chapter is for you. It suggests not only how you can live with their demands but also how you can encourage them toward change.

Recognizing that it can be a real nuisance to live with a perfectionist, let's change the word *perfectionist* into a contraction: *pe'st*. Just for fun, okay? Now let's consider how we can get along well with our favorite pe'sts. Pe'st friends can be best friends.

APPROACHES THAT DON'T WORK

For starters, consider some approaches that don't work. It won't help either of you if you are a pest to your pe'st.

1. Giving cheap advice. When is the last time you used cheap advice someone gave to you? Save your breath.

2. Nagging or being a volunteer watchdog. If your pe'st wanted a warden, he or she would go to jail. So don't be a warden. But if you're *invited* to be a watchdog, celebrate that your pe'st is asking for help to be accountable.

3. Complaining to others. Talking in public about your frustrations with your pe'st will only embarrass him or her and create resentment. If you need to talk to someone about it, talk to the pe'st.

4. Hinting about change. Hints about change are wasted on pe'sts. They are convinced that their methods and standards are right.

5. Retaliating. It won't help to iron a large crease down the front of your pe'st husband's T-shirts if you're angry because he wants his T-shirts ironed. Or it won't help to put a dead cricket on the front seat of the car because you're angry that your pe'st wife likes her car spotless.

6. Trying to change the pe'st. Give up every thought that you may be able to change the pe'st. Of all the changes that have been made in your life, was any one of them done *without* you? No. And you can't change your pe'st. You can nudge, encourage, support, assist, but *you* can't change the pe'st.

COPING WITH THE PE'ST WHO DENIES THE NEED TO CHANGE

The pe'st will change when, and only when, he or she decides to change. Until then, use the following methods to help you cope with your pe'st.

1. Look at yourself. Find out if you have been abrasive to the pe'st. If the pe'st has seemed abrasive to you, you probably have returned the disfavor. If you have, clean up the mess by apologizing. Then clean up your act by not doing it any more.

2. Compliment the pe'st. Compliment the pe'st for actions and personal characteristics that have nothing to do with his or her perfectionism. Reassure pe'sts of their intrinsic worth; we all need that. Give praise that says they are valuable apart from performance. Practice this with your favorite pe'st.

3. Reassure the pe'st of your friendship. Pe'sts need to be told that you are still committed to the friendship. Send a card or say that powerful little thing that renews the bond of caring.

4. Help the pe'st understand how his or her behavior affects you. Phrasing your comments as a report, not as a judgment, increases the chance that your concerns will be heard. Compare these two responses: "Your standards of neatness around the house are ridiculous. You're going to drive all of us into the loony bin if you can't relax with one speck of dust in the same room." Or, "I like seeing the house sparkling clean and organized when I come home. Sometimes I think I'd be more comfortable if I had more freedom to let things lie around a little more. Last evening when I was reading a magazine, I dropped it on the floor by my chair when I finished. You asked me to put it back on the coffee table at the other side of the room right away. I think we can enjoy our home and life more with greater freedom on little matters like that."

The first condemns, the second affirms and reports. While the second takes longer, it may lead to progress. But condemnation is sure to make matters worse. Before you say something to your pe'st, prayerfully think it through. You may even want to write out your comments so you are sure you are reporting without condemning.

5. Encourage the pe'st to talk about his or her perfectionism. Ask the pe'st to tell you how he or she benefits by perfectionistic striving. For example, you could say to your pe'st, "I know you work very hard to keep your car clean inside and out all the time. Because I want to know and understand you better, please tell me, if you'd like to, how you benefit from all that good effort." Show genuine interest and listen to the response. As the pe'st responds, he or she may even begin to question the value of the behavior you have questioned. Be gentle and nonjudgmental. Let the person come to his or her own conclusions.

6. Concentrate on your own growth into the image of Christ. Romans 3:23 says, "All have sinned and fall short of the glory of God." That's you and me! We continue to fall short of perfection, even after our sins are forgiven. One of the best gifts we can give our pe'st friends is a friend who is conforming to the image of Jesus Christ. Consider if you are sufficiently active in the disciplines that bring spiritual growth: worship, fellowship, prayer, quiet time, and study. If not, change it.

SUPPORT THE PE'ST WHO WANTS TO CHANGE

Pe'sts who want to change must develop their plan for doing so. Here are some ways you can help.

1. Help the pe'st be specific. Pe'sts often want to change everything at once. Help your pe'st identify specific behaviors or thoughts that need to change. Don't make the list for the pe'st, but help him or her phrase goals that are realistic and measurable.

It is vague, for instance, to say, "I'll not try so hard to write a perfect letter." Instead, state the goal so it can be measured: "I'll write the best letter I can as a rough draft. I'll look at it an hour later and make any changes I want to, then type and mail it." The latter plan is definite and easy to follow or not follow.

2. Don't reinforce behavior that the pe'st has agreed is unreasonable. If your pe'st friend measures and draws lines on an envelope to make sure she sticks the stamp on straight, ignore it or question it; don't say "I'll bet the postmaster general wishes everyone would be so neat." You have a right to question this behavior only if the pe'st has asked for your help in changing it.

3. Ask the pe'st how you can be helpful. The pe'st is likely to be pleased by your concern and willingness to help if you're not judgmental or impatient. Let the pe'st take the lead because he or she is the best person to suggest how you *can* help.

4. Listen. Let the pe'st know that you are willing to listen about anything. The pe'st will face discouragements, setbacks, and victories. Be open to listening attentively in all of these situations. And remember to listen without finding fault.

5. Pray. Intercede for the person in prayer. If the person is comfortable with it, pray together about the changes he or she is working on, praising God for the growth and asking for his continued help with the difficulties.

WHEN YOUR BOSS IS A PE'ST

You are much more limited in resources and privileges in trying to reshape a job supervisor who is a pe'st. The best approach you can take is to capitalize on your supervisor's desire for you to be productive.

Suppose the supervisor wants you to do an exceptional job on task A, but doing that will interfere with completing task B. You might say, "I understand what you want me to do with task A, but I'm also concerned about task B. I wonder, should I give attention to B before putting the finishing touches on A?"

It is more tactful to raise your objections by asking questions because questions leave the supervisor in the position of being the expert (whether or not the person is one). Phrase your concerns in a way that shows your desire to contribute to the supervisor's goals and effectiveness.

14

Perfectionism and Parenting

The bad news: To date, no parent has been perfect.

Look at some Old Testament parents. Isaac and Rebekah certainly wouldn't get high marks for their management of the sibling rivalry between Jacob and Esau. Jacob, whose sons sold their brother Joseph into slavery, certainly couldn't apply for the perfect parent award. And think about Adam and Eve; they must have doubted their parenting skills when they learned that Cain had killed his brother Abel. Having a tough time raising children is nothing new.

The good news: Parents don't need to be perfect.

I'm optimistic about the parenting process. When parents truly love their children and communicate that love, the things they do right will be powerful enough to compensate for the normal omissions and excesses on the negative side. In time, love prevails over mistakes.

If you are a parent of young children, concentrate on knowing your children fully, without prejudging what their interests and preferences will be. Do all that you can to communicate unqualified love. Concentrate on relating to your children in ways that imitate God's love to you.

Suggestions like the ones in this chapter are valuable, but without love they are nothing.

If you are a parent nearing empty-nest time, don't chastise yourself for mistakes you have made in parenting. Continue to love your children. Develop an adult-to-adult relationship that enables you to talk about anything with your children.

This doesn't ignore the fact that almost everyone comes into adult life with a few unhealed wounds from their experiences with their parents. But clumsiness in parenting can only be reduced, not eliminated. Parents who try to be perfect or who try to raise perfect children may inflict more damage on their children than parents who take a more casual approach.

PARENTS AND PERFECTIONISM

Perfectionism and parenting mix in several ways. First, parents may try to be perfect in their own lives. Second, parents may want their children to be perfect. Third, children may strive for perfection for their own reasons. Let's look at each of these patterns.

PARENTS WHO TRY TO BE PERFECT

Parents who demand perfection from themselves are almost certain to pass on those demands to the people around them, especially to their children. If the parents reward the children vigorously for high performance, the pattern of perfectionism is ever-present and reinforced. The children may become perfectionists for survival, if for no other reason.

When children see their parents imposing perfectionistic standards on themselves, the children may learn a perfectionistic style by modeling their parents' behavior, even if the parents don't require it. If perfectionistic parents don't praise their children, the children probably will assume that they need to be perfect, just as the parents are trying to be perfect. The children may become perfectionists just to gain approval. When these children become adults, they are likely to develop into dependent "people pleasers," still seeking the pats on the head they never received during childhood.

Or the children may rebel. They may be perfectionists in one area—taking care of the baseball-card collection or the doll's clothing—but rebellious in matters that annoy the parents—having a messy room or dressing sloppily. Remember that Odelia (chapter 7) rebelled extensively because of her mother's perfectionism.

PARENTS WHO WANT THEIR CHILDREN TO BE PERFECT

Parents who want their children to be perfect often withhold approval. Children may respond to this environment by trying all the harder to perform well—just to receive affirmation. This was the situation Nels faced (chapter 7); Nels spent most of his adult life working hard to earn his father's praise or approval.

Sometimes parents praise children only for a certain level of performance. In rewarding only perfect performance, parents almost force children to become perfectionists. The more the "perfect behavior" is reinforced, the more the perfectionism becomes part of some children's personality style.

In either of these situations the children will pay the price for perfectionistic living. They may become aware that the costs outweigh the benefits, and when they realize that the burden began with parental expectations, they may rebel.

Such was the case with Xavier. When Xavier entered a state-wide competition in Latin mythology, he earned the second highest score among the 750 competitors. Rather than congratulate her son for his victory, Xavier's mother said to him, "If only you had studied a little harder, you could have won first place."

His father responded similarly: "Son, you were goofing off. I tried to get you to study, but you just wouldn't. Now look how unhappy you have made your mother." No congratulations, no celebration, no whoopee, just "if only" and a guilt trip.

So when Xavier went to college that fall, he spent most of his time shooting pool and playing video games. This was his way of saying, "If winning second place isn't good enough for you, why should I bother to do anything?"

When parents try to fulfill their own ambitions through the accomplishments of their children, they will give the child many messages that encourage perfectionistic striving. "Always do your best." "See if you can do better next time." "If you had tried harder, you could have done better." These statements may have merit, but when they are coupled with conditions in the relationship, they are deadly.

"Always do your best" is a nice little cliché. It might even be inspiring. But when it is said with this statement, "You didn't do your best this time," the child hears, "I don't like you as well as I would if you had performed better. So if you want my love in the future, you must perform better." Loving parents don't say things like this on purpose; it seeps out through nonverbal signals and enters the child's interpretations (some correct, some incorrect).

CHILDREN WHO WANT TO BE PERFECT

Children will try to be perfect because they are trying to gain rewards, to avoid criticism, or to bring order out of chaos. In any case, perfectionistic behavior is a symptom of unhealthy conditions in the family. Take it seriously as a symptom.

PERFECTIONISM AND FIRST-BORN CHILDREN

The first child enters a family that is different from the one his or her siblings may enter: it has no other children. The first-born child is a "solo star." This star status carries some privileges: the parents are very attentive and quick to respond, convinced that their child can do no wrong. The child has no brat brother or sister to compete with, to be disrupted by, or to share the toys with. What a life the first-born child usually has!

First-born children learn more rules, are taught to be more systematic, and are given lots of encouragement to be perfect. The expectations are high. The baseball glove is waiting in the crib when the little guy arrives home from the hospital; baby daughter gets a Miss America layette. Perfectionists are in the making.

HELP YOUR CHILD AVOID THE PERFECTIONISM TRAP

If you're a perfectionist and like it, then keep doing what got you here and your kids will be the same. But if you want to help your children know the thrill of excellence instead of the agony of perfectionism, take a better road. For example:

1. Give approval and reward in proportion to your children's efforts. When your children work hard on a project, encourage them. Emphasize effort rather than performance.

2. Ask the difficult, not the impossible. Challenge your children to do hard tasks, but don't ask the impossible from them. Help them enjoy the thrill of accomplishing something they thought they couldn't do, but don't put unrealistic expectations on them.

3. When correcting children, report, don't demand. Children are more likely to listen to your objections if they are stated as reports, not as criticisms. Which of these responses is a child more likely to hear? "You shouldn't have spent so much time making a fancy cover for that report. All that meticulous work is just time wasted. You don't show the teacher that you learned anything by doing fancy artwork on the report cover. Because of wasting all that time, you're going to flunk algebra." Or, "The cover is very attractive and certainly shows your artistic talent. I have some concern that by spending so much time on the cover, you may be neglecting your algebra homework. How is that coming along?"

4. Emphasize the adventure of the process, not just the end result. A few days ago I went hiking around a nearby lake and stopped to talk with a grizzled man who was pulling his boat out of the water. "How was fishing?" I asked.

"Didn't catch a thing today. Got a bunch last week, but nothing today."

"But did you have fun?"

He smiled from ear to ear. "Oh, sure! It was a great day. You know," he said, "a bad day fishing is better than a good day doing anything else."

Fishing is a joyous and rewarding process for that happy man. Catching a fish is optional.

5. Draw a limit on the perfectionistic striving when it's extreme. Late one night my daughter was frantic about a junior-high homework assignment. She had worked several hours already, it was late, and she said tearfully that she had to work on it for several hours more. I forbade her to work on it, and she went to bed somewhat disgruntled by my dictate.

Why was I insistent? In my judgment she was exaggerating both the importance of the assignment and the consequences of handing in a 90-percent paper rather than a 100-percent one. We talked about it the following evening so there would be no lingering tensions. I wanted to learn why doing so well was important to her, and I wanted her to consider my perspective on the issue. It worked out well.

6. Admit your own imperfection. That may be more for your own benefit than for others, who have probably seen your imperfection clearly enough. But it's important for your children to know that you accept imperfection in yourself. Children can accept you as a friend more easily when you are in more human scale to them; let them rub up against you, not just against your pedestal.

7. Don't hesitate to apologize. "Man is never so tall as when he bows to apologize" an early American proverb goes. When your children see you apologize, they learn that it's okay to make mistakes.

8. Remind yourself to free up the first-born child. The oldest child usually gets saddled with more household chores than the younger ones, including baby-sitting them. Do your best to keep this equitable and consistent among the kids. Negotiate and pay for extra duties such as baby-sitting (an opportunity to teach work and money habits at the same time).

9. Be patient with your children—and yourself. Perfectionists, whether children or adults, are sensitive to criticism. They need to learn to take criticism, but children deserve patience from their parents. Teach them to pursue excellence instead of perfection, to find as much joy in doing as in "done," to be charitable with themselves in failure, and most of all to know the ultimate experience of acceptance, which is relationship with God.

10. If you are a perfectionist, get over it. One of the finest gifts you can give your child is to be at peace with yourself, for that enables you to set the best example and to be at your best in nurturing them. If you are a parent trying to be perfect, I beg of you on behalf of your children to break the chain of this burden before it goes another generation.

11. Enjoy the process of raising a child. Again, enjoy the process rather than waiting just for the time at which you stand back and admire the finished product. A bad day parenting can be as good as a good day doing anything else.

15

Reap the Joy of Better Living

Once you have broken out of the perfectionism trap, you're free to become complete, effective, and vigorous. By living under God's authority and in partnership with him, you can develop attitudes and abilities far beyond your former limitations.

I was blessed to grow up knowing some people who have done this, tender-hearted people of tough faith, ordinary people of extraordinary vitality in their relationships with God.

From several of these people I have experienced the fruit of the Spirit: love, joy, peace, patience, kindness, goodness, faithfulness, gentleness, and self-control (Gal. 5:22–23). It's enjoyable to visit these people or to leaf through the pages of my memory to learn how they have become shaped into the image of Christ.

It's difficult to imagine one of those friends engaging in any variety of sin, yet when I discuss with them their own perception of their holiness, they are quick to identify sin in their lives. Not obvious sins (like rage, witchcraft, orgies, or others listed in Galatians 5:19–21) but subtle sins of the heart (like conceit, Gal. 5:26) and of omission (like indifference to their opportunities for Christian service, Gal. 6:1–6). They're concerned about these sins, but they aren't debilitated by them.

These people have wonderful balance between their security about God's forgiveness and their awareness that their performance is not ideal. Their dismay over their sins is vivid and motivates self-discipline, but it's balanced by celebration of God's grace. Confidence in God's grace enables their joyous living and prevents the shortfall in performance from interfering with their spiritual growth.

This balance is possible because they love the Lord and are certain of his love for them. Their experience of God's love is as solid as the Bible they daily hold in their hands, as three-dimensional as the place in which they regularly worship. Their joy comes from spending time with him in study and prayer (doing) and by having a heart that is open to change (being).

Instead of listening to bogus beliefs from a mega-voice in the past, they listen to God's voice—past, present, and future—that can speak only truth. Instead of seeking happiness in this world, they find contentment that is a sampling of the joys beyond this world. May we follow their lead.

> Gracious Lord in heaven, mend my divided heart. Reach into every corner, Yahweh, with illumination of your truth and with the power of your healing.
>
> Show me the folly of pursuing perfection. Only you are perfect; my efforts are only self-mockery.
>
> Your love to me is perfect. I can't comprehend it. I don't know why you love me, but I know you do. I thank you for it and for the promise of perfection when, in your time, I meet you face to face.
>
> Until then, guide me in ever-increasing conformity into the pattern of your design, the image of which I have seen in the obedient life, sacrificial death, and triumphant resurrection of your son, Jesus Christ, in whose name I pray. Amen.

Appendix

John Wesley's Footnotes
Orville S. Walters, M.D.

There is confusion among those who profess to enjoy Christian perfection—as well as among those whose acquaintance with the doctrine is more casual—concerning the influence of entire sanctification upon everyday life. It is generally agreed that such an experience should produce some effect upon outward conduct, but much uncertainty prevails concerning the extent of this influence. There is an unfortunate tendency to associate with this Wesleyan doctrine a perfectionism that is quite incompatible with the realities of physiological and psychological function.

The footnotes added by John Wesley to one section of his *Plain Account of Christian Perfection* are a testimony to the author's willingness to bring his earlier writings into harmony with his maturer understanding of human nature. Finding his former expectations unrealistically overstated and incompatible with life in a finite frame, Wesley sharply limited his categorical declarations by adding this series of corrective afterthoughts.

Some of Wesley's earlier expectations for the state of perfect love would have represented a virtual suspension of some physiological adjustments that are essential for man's well-being. One such statement in the *Plain Account* describes the wholly sanctified as free from desire for "ease in pain."

The faculty of pain perception is invaluable for proper function of the body. Although there are many instances in which its relief is desired and produced, pain is the principal indicator of disturbed body function. Because pain may become intolerable, persons are driven to seek alleviation of the condition which is producing pain. Rather than endure pain, we seek to have its cause removed. To lose this action-getting device would leave man without an indispensable protection. Wesley wrote in a later footnote, "This is too strong. Our Lord Himself desired ease in pain., He asked for it, only with resignation, 'Not as I will,' I desire, 'but as thou wilt.'"

Fear is another important alarm-sounder. While fear may become a liability, the adjustments which accompany fear are important in meeting the emergencies of life. There are automatic adjustments produced throughout the body that are triggered by fear. It is quite unthinkable that the grace of perfect love should abolish this physiological device that mobilizes body resources in emergencies. Having written earlier concerning those who have entered the state of Christian perfection, "They have no fear or doubt, either as to their state in general, or as to any particular action," Wesley later amended the statement by appending, "Frequently this is the case, but only for a time."

Wesley also described the wholly-sanctified person as one who has in prayer "no thought of anything past, or absent, or to come, but of God alone." This surprising description denies the universal tendency for associative thought process to occur spontaneously and more or less continuously during waking hours. We may focus our thinking through conscious effort, but we can control the flow only within narrow limits.

Wesley later reconciled his earlier view with psychological reality by adding the footnote, "This is far too strong." His sermon "On Wandering Thoughts," adds, "To avoid these, we must go out of the world."

Regarding intellectual functions, the *Plain Account* further states, "The 'unction from the Holy One' teaches them every hour what they shall do, and what they shall speak; nor have they therefore any need to reason concerning it." The unhappy result of practicing a proposition so fallacious, or his maturer consideration, led the great founder to add later, "sometimes they have no need; at other times they have."

There are occasions, Christians believe, when they may enjoy the illumination which comes from the Holy Spirit's prompting, called by E. Stanley Jones, "the inner Voice." Many of mature years in the Christian life have on occasion been conscious of such leading. The preponderance of testimony, however, indicates that clear-cut inward leading is often lacking, and one must frequently draw upon his reasoning ability, intelligence and experience, supplemented by the wise counsel of others, to steer the right course.

Indeed, one may occasionally be perplexed, not only by lack of specific guidance, but by obsessions which masquerade as divine leading, and which eventually can be overcome only by the marshalling of solid intellectual argument or evidence which reveals the unsoundness of the recurrent idea.

Some who lack the later insight of Wesley still profess to be living under the specific and minute direction of the Holy Spirit, thereby claiming for themselves immunity not only from errors of judgment, but also from criticism or correction by their fellows.

If Wesley's first rash conclusions regarding reason were true, there would no longer be any use for the reasoning capacity of the wholly sanctified. They would be persons without individuality, for they would not determine their own thoughts and actions. Their intellectual processes would be entirely superseded by divine direction. Such a condition does not square either with experience or God's way of working.

When sin is defined as the willful transgression of a known law, the degree of Christian excellence achieved in conduct depends in part upon increasing one's knowledge. In order to do better, we need to know more, hence growth in Christian grace calls for cultivation of the intellect. It is unthinkable that an experience of deepening Christian grace should ever lead to suspension of submergence of normal intellectual function.

Susceptibility to temptation is another common human characteristic not abolished by the grace of Christian perfection. "They are in one sense freed from temptation," reads Wesley's *Plain Account of Christian Perfection,* "for though numberless temptations fly about them, yet they trouble them not." The great Wesley must have experienced some such triumphant period, but the footnote added later reads, "Sometimes they do not; at other times they do, and that grievously."

Just as one might live free from all errors of judgment without having to think, if supernatural leading were always available, he might also live free from all moral wrong without having to choose, if temptation were eliminated. In the first case, intellectual choice would be superseded; in the second case, moral choice would be superseded.

Neither proposition harmonizes with the facts of human experience, nor with the biblical description of man's nature. So long as he lives, man has freedom to choose evil in preference to good if he wills to do so. Temptation is the presentation of a plausible incitement to choose evil. "Demas hath forsaken me, having loved this present world. . . . Luke is with me." The descendants of Demas as well as those of Luke are still numerous.

Many of the inherited characteristics of personality are unmodified by Christian experience; the same may be said of many acquired behavior patterns which are the result of habitual response to certain stimuli or situations.

"The Lord may forgive us our sins, but the nervous system never does." This statement was born of the keen insight and observation of a man who had an uncommon knowledge both of Christian experience and of the nervous system about which he wrote. An inadequate understanding of what William James saw clearly has been the cause of much difficulty to religious people both before and since his day.

When sin is forgiven, the guilt attendant upon the transgression of God's laws is resolved in the process, but long-continued practices of gratification or indulgence leave a deeply-grooved tracery. The ineradicability of the record stored in the neural archives is well illustrated by memory, which requires only suitable association for recall. It is true that "the expulsive power of a new affection" may dominate or submerge these ingrained tendencies, but the conduct patterns of sinful living are written into the nervous system as indelibly as memory itself.

If the record of sin remains in the nervous system, so does the record of a sanctified life. Wrong choices, often repeated, shape the personality, but so do right choices and life devoted to the practice of Christian love in action. Just as the personality which chooses evil becomes more and more firmly fixed in a rigid mold of its own fashioning, the life wholly committed to Christ develops and flowers progressively. The attainment of Christian maturity is a process which lasts as long as life and is characterized by progressive and gradual advancement in outward approximation to the Christian ideal.

This is to say, in other words, that a Christian may be wholly sanctified in an instant, but he will need years of growth in grace to achieve stability and maturity in Christian character, a fact of which Wesley was well aware. "At all times their souls are even and calm," he wrote at first; "their hearts are steadfast, and immovable." The footnote, added later, reads, "Not all who are saved from sin. Many of them have not attained it yet."

A latter-day holiness preacher, whose ministry partook more of zeal than of learning, is reported to have exclaimed upon reading Wesley's footnotes in the *Plain Account,* "Who put those there? Why, they spoil the whole thing!" From its beginning to the present, the Wesleyan movement has had enthusiastic advocates whom, missing the force of the founder's revisions, have retraced the same painful extravagances, only to arrive at a dead end of frustration for themselves, undeserved guilt and confusion for their people, and discredit for the movement. John Wesley's footnotes attest clearly the evolution in his thought from an unrealistic perfectionism, to a perfection-in-love; from a fixed standard of outward performance, to a dynamic inner relationship with Christ.

Notes

Chapter 1

[1] Items 9 and 18 are scored higher because of the importance of parental influence. Item 14 is scored differently because of the way in which it is worded.

Chapter 2

[1] A more complete explanation of human motivation may be found in chapter 3 of my book *Counseling for Problems of Self-Control* (Waco, Tex.: Word, 1987).

[2] *American Psychiatric Association: Diagnostic and Statistical Manual of Mental Disorders,* third edition, revised (Washington, D.C.: American Psychiatric Association, 1987).

Chapter 4

[1] See "John Wesley's Footnotes," *The Free Methodist* (May 15, 1963). For a more complete, scholarly work on this subject, see O. S. Walters' "John Wesley's Footnotes to Christian Perfection," *Methodist History* (October, 1973).

[2] John Wesley, *A Plain Account of Christian Perfection,* In: Thomas Jackson, *The Works of John Wesley* (London: Wesleyan Methodist Book House, 1872), Vol. XI, pp. 366–446. In *A Plain Account of Christian Perfection,* Wesley introduces an excerpt from his earlier book, *The Character of a Methodist,* with the statement, "In this I described a perfect Christian," and calls attention to a disclaimer on its title page, "Not as though I had already attained."

Chapter 5

[1] Hans Walter Wolff, *Anthropology of the Old Testament* (Philadelphia: Fortress, 1973), pp. 40–55.

[2] I have found Dr. Gary R. Sweeten's teaching on this topic to be very helpful. Tapes and a workbook titled *Breaking Free*

From the Past are available from Christian Information Committee, P. O. Box 24080, Cincinnati, OH 45224.

Chapter 7

[1]Depression often is caused and/or aggravated by biochemical factors. In those cases, appropriate pharmacological treatment is often helpful or necessary. I arranged for Nels to be evaluated by a psychiatrist, who concluded that antidepressant medication was not needed.

Chapter 8

[1]I chose progressive tense (*ing* forms) for the harmonizing heart and the dividing heart to emphasize the active nature of human process. The term *harmonized heart* might lead us to think that it just sits there in splendor, never changing, like a gloriously fashioned museum piece. No, it influences everything in and around the heart. And if it doesn't resist the contamination of sin, it's subject to degenerate into a dividing heart. We must keep in mind the importance of continued maintenance of the harmonizing heart.

Chapter 10

[1]I am indebted to David D. Burns for this technique, adapted from his book *Feeling Good* (New York: William Morrow, 1980). I also thank several clients whose use of the method vividly demonstrated its usefulness.